To my kids, who inspire me. A.M.

First published in Great Britain 2022 by Red Shed, part of Farshore
An imprint of HarperCollins*Publishers*
1 London Bridge Street, London SE1 9GF
www.farshore.co.uk

HarperCollins*Publishers*
1st Floor, Watermarque Building, Ringsend Road
Dublin 4, Ireland

Text copyright © Ant Middleton 2022.
Ant Middleton has asserted his moral rights.
Illustrations © HarperCollins*Publishers 2022*
Cover photograph © Pål Hansen 2022
Cat artwork page 50/153 and target artwork (throughout) © Shutterstock 2022

Consultancy by Dr Miquela Walsh, DEdPsych, MsC (Dist), BSc (Hons), HCPC accredited.

ISBN 978 0 7555 0381 0
Printed and Bound in the UK using 100% Renewable Electricity at CPI Group (UK) Ltd.
001
A CIP catalogue record for this title is available from the British Library.

Stay safe online. Any website addresses listed in this book are correct at the time of going to print.
However, Farshore is not responsible for content hosted by third parties. Please be aware that online
content can be subject to change and websites can contain content that is unsuitable for children.
We advise that all children are supervised when using the internet.

Farshore takes its responsibility to the planet and its inhabitants very seriously.
We aim to use papers from well-managed forests by responsible suppliers.

MISSION TOTAL RESILIENCE

ANT MIDDLETON

RED SHED

CONTENTS

INTRODUCTION

I'm Ant Middleton. You might have seen me on the television, jumping out of helicopters and running around like my pants are on fire. I spend my life doing cool stuff. I've climbed Mount Everest, I've travelled to the jungle and the desert – to some of the wildest, most extreme parts of the world! I was a soldier, taking on some of the most dangerous, demanding challenges possible.

But if you'd told me when I was a kid that I'd end up doing *any* of these things, I wouldn't have believed you. I wasn't born brave. I was a small, sensitive child who didn't know how to stay still. Most of all, I was a bit timid and afraid of making mistakes. I remember how intimidating so much of the world seemed to me. Stuff happened – like my father dying and our whole family relocating to another country – and I felt overwhelmed.

But I've learned a lot since then, and I wanted to share all of it with you. I know now that life throws all sorts at us, but that it's possible to take anything, no matter how upsetting, in your stride, and maybe even turn it to your advantage. I've learned that you can overcome adversity, and that it's OK to fail. Which is a long way of saying that I've seen that it's possible to build RESILIENCE.

But what is resilience? Different people will give you different answers. Here's mine.

RESILIENCE IS A MIXTURE OF CONFIDENCE IN YOURSELF, EMOTIONAL CONTROL AND EXPERIENCE.

Those things are all great by themselves. If you put them all together, it's like having a super-power.

When you're resilient, you find that there's not much in life that fazes you. Bad things will come along, but you'll be able to cope with them. Resilience is what helps you get back on your feet when you've had a setback. It can help make you self-reliant. You'll find that you're able to solve stuff without always having to ask for help from the adults in your life, or your older brother or sister. You'll feel willing to try new skills and challenges, even when the mere idea of them makes you feel a bit nervous. You'll be able to keep going when times get tough and there's a little voice in your head telling you it would be easier to give up.

Confidence means that you'll know you have the strength and the tools to manage whatever it is you're facing. You'll have accepted who you are and what you're capable of. And you'll understand that you matter, and that people will listen to you when you need them to.

Emotional control means that, when you find yourself confronted by challenging things, you can control how you respond (both internally and externally).

Experience means that every time something that feels tough or difficult occurs (which it will), and you survive it (which in time you will, even if it feels almost impossible now), you'll be even stronger afterwards. How cool is that?

But I also think it's possible to start building resilience without sitting around waiting for disaster to strike. You could think of it like the muscles in your body. If you don't exercise, your muscles won't grow. But if you play sports or go to the gym or even run up and down your street 5,000 times a day (I don't recommend the last one), then you'll get stronger and stronger. It's the same with resilience. **The more you do stuff, the more you open yourself up, and the more resilient you can become.** I hope that by the time you've turned the last page of this book, that's exactly what you'll be raring to do!

I wish I'd had a book like this when I was growing up. It's not academic and there aren't any complex ideas. I'm a doer. I'm a fidget with the attention span of a gnat. I'm hyperactive. And that's how I get better at anything. I find out what I can, then I go and try it. I might make a mess of it, I might not, but I know that doesn't matter. Experience is an amazing teacher. So none of the lessons in these pages come from a classroom. They're the result of everything that I've seen and done, everything that's happened to me. I've made stupid mistakes. I've tripped myself up more times than I care to mention. I've failed over and over again. But my advice is tried and tested. It's what works for me. It works for all the grown-ups I help. And I think it will work for you. You might find it demanding at times, but I guarantee it will be worth it. I think it will also be a lot of fun.

One last thing.

YOU'RE STRONGER THAN YOU THINK YOU ARE.

You're probably pretty resilient already. I mean, flipping heck, you've lived through a global pandemic! I'm only here to help you find what's already inside you.

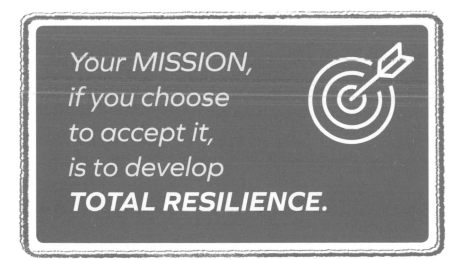

Your MISSION, if you choose to accept it, is to develop TOTAL RESILIENCE.

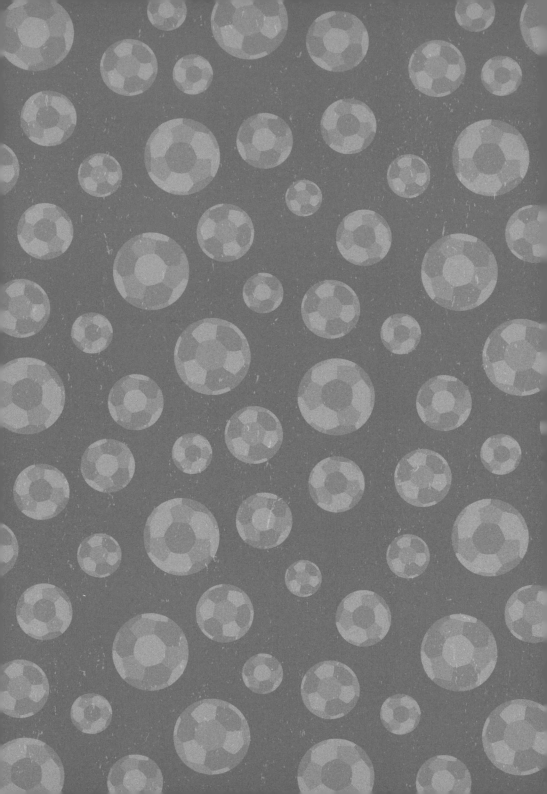

CHAPTER ONE

LIFE CAN GET TOUGH

You don't need me to tell you that life is full of things you probably wish weren't there. There's the stuff you know about, like exam stress and bullies and losing important games of football. And then there are those curveballs, the things that just come out of nowhere. Like lockdowns, or suddenly discovering that you're going to have to move to another city.

When I was barely eight years old my dad died. That, I can tell you, was a curveball!

One moment I was a normal kid going to a normal school in a normal town in England. The next thing I knew I'd lost my father. It wasn't something I ever could have anticipated.

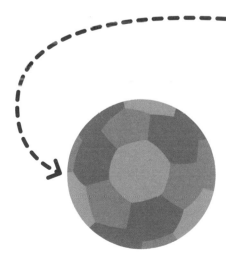

I didn't have time to prepare for it. But, blimey, suddenly I had to deal with it.

You might have experienced something similar, you might not. If you have, I'm truly sorry. I was devastated by the loss. Suddenly there was this yawning gap in my life. There were days when I didn't think I'd survive the pain. It seemed to live permanently beneath my ribs.

Things got even more complicated when my mum re-married. Every detail about Dad was wiped from our lives. Even his picture was taken off the walls.

And then, quite suddenly, we moved to France. We went from a hectic life in Portsmouth to a remote village in Normandy, where a lost cow or a very fat chicken could end up as the talk of the town. It was a big jolt.

To begin with, there was a period of freedom when I could run wild in the fields around our home. We had adventures, built dens, it was amazing. But it couldn't last. I had to go to school, which felt like a very bad thing to me. Nobody likes being the new kid, right? And as if I wasn't nervous enough, I wasn't just going into a new school: I was going to a new school in a new country where they spoke a language I didn't understand. Nightmare!

Somehow, there was space for the situation to get worse. On my first day, my mum's rackety old car wouldn't start, so we were seriously late. I remember how embarrassed I was as, watched by twenty very curious kids and one very cranky teacher, I walked into the classroom. Then, just as I was thinking, *Well, at least this is as bad as it will get*, something else happened. I tried to explain why we were late, mumbling the few mangled words of French my brothers had taught me on the car ride in. It turns out I accidentally said something *very* rude. (Too rude for this book – I wanted to put it in, but I was told I'd get into trouble if I did.) The entire room started laughing at me. My cheeks became even redder and even hotter. Those seconds seemed to me like some of the hardest I'd ever had to face. They left me feeling really shaken, even a bit frightened.

At break-time, all the French boys and girls crowded around me. I was a weirdo to them. It must have been like a Martian had just appeared. They asked a million questions that I couldn't understand. I felt so nervous and confused that even though I was really hungry, I didn't dare go to the cafeteria. I just found somewhere to hide. I crouched down and asked myself, over and over,

'WHAT THE *FLIP* IS GOING ON?'

As soon as we got home that afternoon, I scrambled into the den my brothers and I had made in the massive tree ferns at the bottom of the garden. I curled up there, counting the cars that whooshed along on the main road that ran past our house. It felt safe there, as if I was protected from all the things that worried and upset me.

WHAT I WANTED
WAS FOR SOMEBODY
TO COME IN WITH A

MAGIC WAND

AND FIX

EVERYTHING

FOR ME.

AND YET I KNEW
THAT WASN'T GOING
TO HAPPEN.

My mum and stepdad had the power to take us back to England. I didn't. I was just a kid. Whether I liked it or not (and I really didn't), I was going to have to keep going to that school.

As I sat there in my den, I thought about my situation. What really helped was reminding myself that, despite all the changes that had exploded into my life, there was some stuff that had stayed the same. I had lost my dad, but my family was still around me. I was surrounded by people who cared for me. I knew that I could always rely on my mum to support me. Whatever else happened, she'd be there with a hug and a smile. I wouldn't have to deal with all of this alone.

We should never underestimate the importance of our family and friends. They help us celebrate the happy moments in life. But they also can help us get through the times that feel tough or challenging.

Take a couple of moments to consider the people who support and believe in you. Then try to think of ways that you can show them how much you appreciate everything they do.

As well as reassuring me, my mum also helped me realise that I could either be that kid who hid away at lunchtime every single day, or I could embrace the situation.
I couldn't transport myself back to Portsmouth, but **I could control how I responded to the environment I was in.**

What was the point of beating myself up about stuff that wasn't in my hands? As soon as I told myself that, I could feel the weight lifting from my shoulders. I knew I wouldn't be late for school every day, and I reckoned that if I was friendly and open with the French children, they'd be friendly and open back. But I also knew I couldn't learn French overnight, so I told myself I wouldn't get dispirited if to begin with I struggled with the language.

The next day I went into school almost without a care in the world. **I stopped worrying and my attitude became far more, *Let's just see how this goes.***
I went into lunch and realised that the food was actually decent. In fact, it was a lot nicer than the school dinners we'd been given in Portsmouth. I played football in the yard with the other children and began to form a connection with them.

The idea of learning French seemed as impossible as becoming a flamingo or growing a new head, but I actually picked up the language quickly. I was surrounded by it, so I didn't really have to try. Within three months I was holding perfect conversations. Within six months I had a Normandy accent. Some people refused to believe I was English.

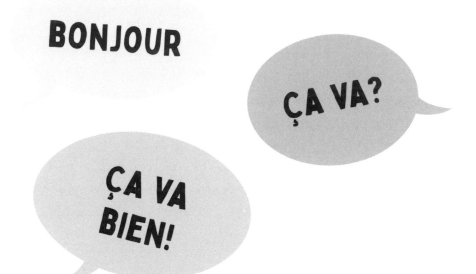

The thing I learned during this period is that sometimes life throws things at you that make you feel uncomfortable or upset. As much as you might want to, that's something you can't avoid. Sometimes these things will be tragedies, like your parent dying; at other times they're smaller challenges, like a first day at school, or an exam.

The only ways to avoid these difficult things are to:

1. Exist in a fantasy world where you pretend that everything is always going to be fine (an absolutely flawless plan . . . until life comes and gives you a big kick up the bum)

2. Stay in your bedroom for ever (which might seem like a good idea at first, but you'll miss out on all the brilliant stuff too).

Acknowledging that sometimes life is going to contain rough patches is important. It's the first step on the way to making sure you can survive them. If you aren't willing to think about the idea that sometimes there are going to be bumps in the road, how are you ever going to prepare for the moment when you end up tripping over one of those bumps?

And when you've been through times that feel tough, it makes you appreciate the moments when it feels like everything is going well even more. It means you don't take stuff for granted. It's only when you're feeling poorly that you remember how brilliant it is to be healthy. It's because I know that life isn't going to be plain sailing that **I try to make sure I recognise and celebrate the good things that happen.**

It is possible to get through difficult moments. And over time, I've learned that you can find ways to help you cope better. More than that, **you can use those tough moments to help you thrive and grow.**

The experience of moving to France felt frightening and uncomfortable at the time, but it taught me a great deal about myself. It showed me that it was possible to get through situations like these, so perhaps I had more inner strength (I didn't know at the time you could also call it resilience) than I'd thought. And there was other stuff too. I never would have thought it would be possible to learn a language as quickly as I did. Discovering that capacity made me more confident.

There's one moment, a few months after we'd arrived, that I'll always remember. By then I'd begun to fit in at school. I could speak the language and had made new friends. The loss of my dad still made me sad, but otherwise life felt good.

WOW,

I THOUGHT TO MYSELF,

I'VE GOT THROUGH THIS.

When we're faced by situations that feel tough or upsetting it can seem overwhelming. But there's an exercise you can do to get your thoughts flowing in a different direction.

1. *Ask yourself, How are you feeling?*
   When I was a kid in France I was afraid that people would laugh at me if I stumbled and made mistakes while trying to speak French.

2. *Name what that worry makes you want to do.*
   All I wanted to do was hide in my den away from everybody else.

The exciting bit is what comes next. This is where you can change that negative thought into a positive one.

3. *Instead of imagining a disaster scenario,*
    try to imagine what it would look like
    if things went well.
    For me that was telling myself, I'll try
    speaking a bit of French and people will
    cheer me for doing my best and giving
    it a go.

4. *How do you feel when you've adopted*
    this positive perspective?
    It made me feel much more happy and
    confident. I was actually quite excited
    about trying out a few words.

Spend a couple of minutes thinking about stuff
that would normally leave you feeling anxious.
See what happens if you change the way you look
at it. Swap a negative outcome for a positive one.
Try to make this an automatic habit – always
imagining a positive scenario rather than a
negative one. Then you'll have equipped yourself
with an amazing tool that will help you whenever
things begin to feel a bit tricky or too much to
cope with. And if doing this feels hard at first, ask
someone you trust to help you think about it.

You can't pretend life is always easy and fun. But you really don't want to go to the opposite extreme and spend too much time worrying about what *might* happen. You can't predict the future. It's going to be full of surprises. Some will feel like changes for the better, some less so. Be liberated by that thought!

When you've built up resilience you can be confident that you'll be able to handle anything that comes your way. (Don't worry, we'll talk about how to do this later.)

THE IMPORTANT THING IS:

HAVE FAITH IN YOURSELF!

We're so bad at remembering how good we are at dealing with stuff!

The other trap a lot of people fall into is assuming that whatever lies ahead of us is inevitably going to be full of scary things. That's just not true. It could be, sure. But it could also be full of lots of cool stuff. Going to a new school might seem scary. But it's also a chance to make a new best friend, or try out new activities and clubs that weren't available at your old school (like photography or street dancing).

THE MOST IMPORTANT LESSON OF ALL

There are seven billion people on the planet. And every single person is different. Every human being will be good at some things and bad at others. Some will be taller, some will be shorter. There will be a person in your class who will learn how to do algebra faster than anybody else, and yet they won't be able to draw brilliant pictures like your friend who is rubbish at maths can. Lionel Messi might be absolutely amazing at football, but I bet you anything that you'll have skills or talents he doesn't.

It's very often the differences between people that make our relationships fun and interesting. Your mates can probably do stuff you can't. They might have been to places that you haven't. But you can probably do stuff they can't. You might have been to places they haven't.

You're an amazing, unique person. I know that so much about you is brilliant and strong and funny and kind. I also know that you will have imperfections and little faults. **Sometimes you'll slip up and get things wrong. But none of that stops the people around you from loving you.** I know that I'm still the same person whether I'm riding high or have just had a massive setback. **I'm more than my failures, just as I'm more than my successes.** The same is true of you. You might have got a couple of steps wrong in a dance routine, or made a mess of an English test, but they only form a very small part of your identity.

SO EMBRACE AND ACCEPT THE INCREDIBLE PERSON

YOU ARE.

CELEBRATE WHAT MAKES YOU SPECIAL AND DIFFERENT!

Make peace with what you can't change, and resolve to improve what you can change. Because when you've done that, you'll already be a lot closer to being the awesomely resilient person I know you can become.

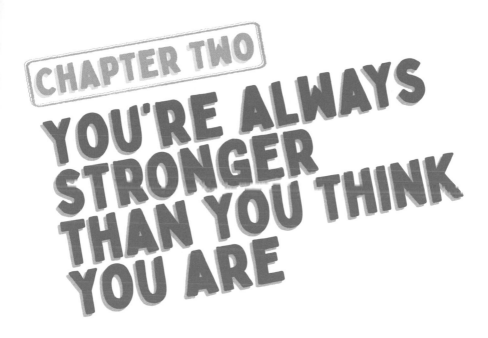

CHAPTER TWO

YOU'RE ALWAYS STRONGER THAN YOU THINK YOU ARE

Do you know the thing that really, really, really frustrates me? The thing that makes me tear my beard out, jump up and down, and shout a lot?

People just don't know what they're capable of. They're in denial. It happens all the time on my television show. A recruit will swear that they can't hold on for a single second longer. Inside, I want to shout, 'Aaaaaargh, not again!' Instead, I'll tell them they CAN stay in that cold water, they CAN keep running. And guess what? They do. It's in there; often it just needs somebody to point it out.

You are stronger than you think you are.

All you need is a key to help unlock all of that. And I'm here to hand it to you.

I like to think I'm pretty resilient these days. There's not much that worries me. There's not much I don't feel I can cope with. I've been to war, I've climbed Everest during the stormy season. I've sailed through the Pacific ocean on a stupidly small wooden canoe, with only a tiny amount of water and some very dry biscuits to keep me going (it's a long story – I'll share it with you later). But I haven't always been like that.

I wasn't a confident kid. I was actually quite sensitive and shy. So when I think back to the nervous, skinny lad I once was, I sometimes ask myself, 'How the flip did I get here?'

There are lots of answers, but here are two that I think are relevant. They made a big difference to me, and I'm confident they can do the same for you. Even better, they're good news! Firstly:

YOU ALREADY ARE RESILIENT!

I don't care who you are or where you're from or what you've done. I don't care how clever you are, or how tall, or what colour your hair is. None of that matters. You've already got a core of resilience inside you.

I'm not just saying this to make you feel better. Remember, I'm the big chief instructor, I'm tough, I tell it like it is. I'm saying it because it's true.

Here's a quick test. Think back over the last couple of years. Make a list of five things that you've found tricky or have upset you. It doesn't matter if they're big or small. Maybe it was missing your friends during lockdown, or one of your favourite pets died, or perhaps it was a teacher shouting at you for messing about.

Do you know what connects all these things (apart from that they happened to you)? YOU SURVIVED THEM! You might not have enjoyed them. They might have made you unhappy or sad. But you got through them. That proves you already are resilient.

I didn't think I was resilient when I was young. But I was already a lot tougher than I imagined.

I'd survived the time after my father died and we'd moved to France. That's not to say that I don't think I could have done better, but I got through it. And just the fact of understanding that helped every time I was faced with adversity afterwards.

I had ended up loving my time in France. I even joined a local football academy and was thinking about becoming a professional footballer. But by my mid-teens I realised I also had a massive desire to explore the world. I wanted adventures and, as pretty as that part of Normandy was, it was also very, very quiet. I knew that eventually I would have to leave. So, after a lot of thought and discussion with my family, I decided to join the British military when I was seventeen. I remember the day I walked through the door of the Army's training centre. The soldiers I met were shocked by how polite and nice I was. They thought my French accent was funny and a few of them even made fun of me. It was a terrifying experience. My family was on the other side of the sea and suddenly I was beginning to wonder if I'd made the right decision to come here.

I'd really wanted to join the Army, but now there was a little voice inside my head saying, 'You can quit. Just turn around and retrace your footsteps. You can give up.

Nobody will mind.' It was overwhelming, it felt too much to take on. And then I thought back to my first experience of France almost a decade before. I realised I was a bit stronger now. A bit better at coping. If I'd got through something as tough as my dad dying and being dropped into a new school in a new country, I knew I could cope with pretty much anything else that came my way. I was right to think that! Once I'd walked through that gate and settled in, I really began to thrive. It was tough, there were lots of challenges, but I felt as if my life was expanding. **I was seeing new things, learning new skills, meeting new people.** I was so glad I hadn't turned around and gone back to France.

Next time something unfamiliar or challenging approaches, draw strength by thinking of something you've done that made you really proud. What skills did you use? What does it tell you about how strong and capable you already are?

MISSION

The second point is even more important. Resilience isn't a skill that some people are naturally better at than others and others will never acquire. It's something we can all learn. Even you!

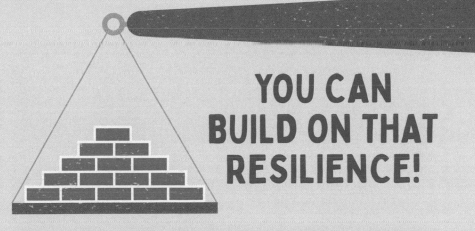

YOU CAN BUILD ON THAT RESILIENCE!

You can take that core of resilience we all have and add all these extra layers and elements to it that will make you even more resilient.

But there's a problem. Lots of us tell stories about ourselves that aren't true. We say, 'Oh, I'm not the sort of person who can do that.' Or 'Oh, I'm just naturally very good at this.' It's very hard for us to shake these convictions.

And these stories hold us back. I know this because, once upon a time, I was the same. For example, I never used to be very good at reading out loud. I used to avoid anything that might involve it. Sometimes I'd end up doing quite elaborate stuff just to escape having to read in public.

The story I told myself was that I was born bad at reading aloud. That's what made me stumble over words. It's also what prevented me from ever trying to get better. I wasn't a natural at reading, so why bother trying!

> **MISSION**
>
> **We're our own worst critics and we're not always able to highlight what we're good at. But the people around us are often much better at seeing how much we're capable of.**
>
> *Step out of your shoes for a moment and try to imagine what a grown-up – like a parent or one of your teachers, or any adult you respect and admire – would say you can do well. Does this change your own view of your abilities?*

It wasn't until my first book came out that I tried to challenge the negative view I had of myself. The publishers asked me if I wanted to narrate the audiobook, or if I'd prefer it if they got an actor in instead. Now, we're not talking a few pages that I could whizz through in minutes. It was a whole flipping book. 70,000 words! I was so tempted to let somebody else do the reading. I cannot tell you how tempted I was.

And then I had a thought, *Do I want to be afraid of this for the rest of my life?* It sounds stupid, but it really bugged me. I realised there was only one option . . .

I got into that recording booth and started reading my book aloud.

It was AGONY.

I had to sit still, which is basically my kryptonite. Sometimes I'd be too close to the microphone and I'd get a shout from the control booth telling me that I was making the mic crackle. Other times I'd be too far away.

I felt like I was terrible at this new task. It seemed to me that I just couldn't get anything right. I'd get flustered and lose my place, there would always be words I struggled to pronounce. If I could get to the bottom of a page without making a mistake, I felt as if I'd won the World Cup. I only managed to finish sixty pages the first day. In eight hours!

Each morning before the recording session I would get into my car full of dread. The thing is, though, I was getting better. The second day I got up to 100 pages. The day after that, 120. It was still really tough, and yet when I measured my progress, **I realised that I'd made a massive step forward.** This made me feel proud, and I began to feel more confident, which in turn meant that I started to enjoy the process. I was still tripping up and getting things wrong the next time I had to do an audiobook, but I knew that I was getting better. And anyway, I reminded myself that even the professional actors who do this sort of thing don't get through every single page without making a few mistakes. (Adults might like to give the impression that we're perfect. Believe me, we're not.) When my third book came around, I found that I was actually looking forward to recording the audio version.

These days I'm reading aloud in public all the time because I'm an ambassador for children's literacy. I do readings of my books to adults too. If you'd asked me to do any of this a few years ago, I'd have jumped out of the window. In my head, I was someone who couldn't read aloud. That was the story I told myself. But I no longer see it that way. I'm still nervous in the seconds before I actually start, and yet I can do it. I open my mouth and the world doesn't end.

Think about picking up any new skill. The first time you try, it's hard. So is the second and third time. After a week or so of practising, you find that you're getting better. **If you carry on working hard, you might end up being awesome.**

RESILIENCE
IS EXACTLY THE SAME.

IT'S NOT ALWAYS EASY, BUT IT IS STRAIGHTFORWARD.

We are problem solvers. It's an essential part of being human and something that's inside all of us. That gift to learn and adapt is what took us from creatures who were just about able to work out how to light a fire by rubbing sticks together, to a species that put men on the moon and developed unfeasibly powerful computers that can fit into our pockets.

But we don't give ourselves credit for how much stuff we pick up. Time for another list!

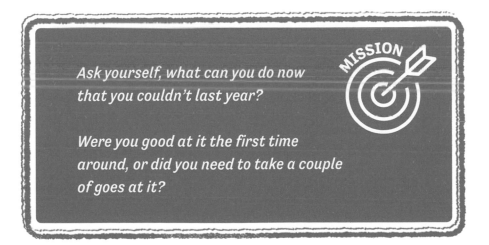

Ask yourself, what can you do now that you couldn't last year?

Were you good at it the first time around, or did you need to take a couple of goes at it?

MISSION

Your brain is like a sponge. It takes in an insane amount of information every single day, especially when you're young. Grown-ups have got ancient brains that are already quite tired and not good at absorbing new things, while your ability to learn is off the scale.

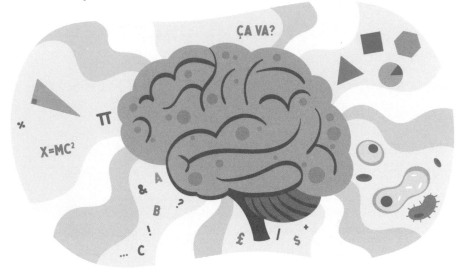

There's nothing fixed about who we are or what we like. We all have an amazing capacity to grow and learn. If you're willing to put in the effort, you can build your confidence in yourself, you can learn how to control your emotions and you can find a way of turning something that seemed like a failure into an opportunity.

So, whenever you find yourself looking at other kids or grown-ups, wondering how they manage to cope when life doesn't go their way and wishing you were like them, remember that YOU CAN DO THIS. As a friend of mine once said to me,

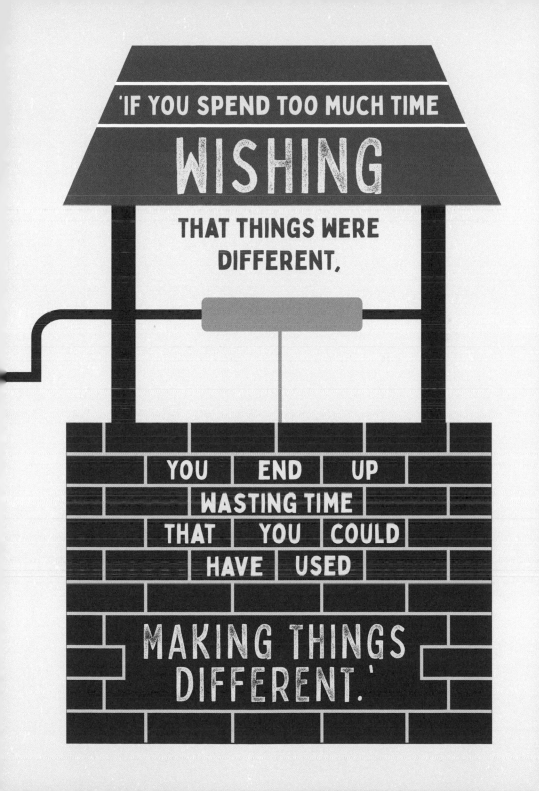

CHAPTER THREE

SMALL BITES, BIG CONFIDENCE

Can I tell you about one of the most frightening moments in my life? It was the spring of 2018. I had just reached the summit of Everest, the tallest mountain in the world, and I couldn't have been any more excited or proud. When I phoned my wife and kids to tell them where I was, I could hardly control my joy. But then a storm began to attack us. The wind was blasting around my head at 70 kilometres per hour, and there was so much snow whipping past me that I could barely see my own hands. I hadn't noticed the icy temperatures much before, but now I realised how brutally cold it was so many thousands of metres high. I could already feel the tingle of frostbite in my fingers and toes.

Other climbers had already started the descent, but because of the chaos caused by the storm it would be another two hours before we could start our own climb down. Suddenly I felt vulnerable and more scared than at any time I could remember. *I'm going to freeze to death,* I thought.

Time slowed to a crawl. Occasionally the flurries of snow would pause for a couple of seconds – long enough for me to take stock of our surroundings – before they began again, even more vicious than before. There was no down or up any more, only white.

'You will die here,' I told myself. I could feel panic gripping every part of my frozen, numbed body. I couldn't even hear my heart beating any more.

But then something changed. I squinted down at my toes, which I could just make out through the blizzard. I realised I could still move them. I was still alive. It felt as if a flame had been reignited inside me.

At that moment I remembered what I was capable of. I reminded myself of all the hours of training and preparation that had led up to this moment. I had climbed several other mountains. I had been an elite military operator. I was fit and strong and healthy. Confidence flooded back into me. 'I can do this,' I told myself. 'I can escape.'

I wasn't alone on Everest. I relied on the help and support provided by people like Ed Wardle, an amazing hybrid of cameraman and adventurer, and Dawa Lama, the best guide to the Himalayas any person could hope for. I wouldn't have got down from that mountain without them.

And that had been the story of the whole journey. I was confident that if ever I needed them, they'd be there for me. I drew strength from just knowing that they had my back and that they believed in me. But I also drew immense strength from the confidence I had in my own abilities. When I was feeling at my lowest, I reminded myself of how much I was capable of and how much I had already achieved. Knowing that gave me the belief to keep going.

CONFIDENCE IS ONE OF THE MOST <u>IMPORTANT</u> ELEMENTS OF **RESILIENCE.**

IF YOU'RE **CONFIDENT,** YOU WILL HAVE FAITH THAT **NO MATTER WHAT LIFE THROWS AT YOU,** YOU'LL BE ABLE TO TAKE IT IN YOUR STRIDE. THE MORE YOU CAN <u>BUILD</u> **YOUR CONFIDENCE,** THE MORE **RESILIENT** <u>YOU WILL</u> BECOME.

And here's the most important thing you need to know:

NOBODY WAS BORN CONFIDENT.

It isn't a natural trait, like the colour of our eyes, or the size of our feet. **Anybody can become confident**, even if it does require a bit of effort. And I promise you it will be worth it!

But before I tell you about that, I need to talk about the two different types of confidence that I think exist. The first is **external confidence,** which depends on what other people think. And then there's **internal confidence,** which is based on your knowledge and acceptance of who you are and what you are capable of.

When your confidence relies on the opinions of other human beings you are always going to be at a disadvantage. You're completely at the mercy of other people's perceptions. It can be very difficult to think one thing about yourself when it feels as if the whole world has a different opinion.

But if you have internal confidence, if you've proved to yourself over and again that you are awesome, you'll find that you're far less affected by setbacks. When something goes wrong, you'll be able to shrug it off because you've got so much under your belt. **If you know your strengths, it's like having a shield.** It doesn't matter how mean other people might be – you can laugh off what they say.

My confidence doesn't depend on what other people say about me. That means that I don't get overly excited when people tell me I'm brilliant and I don't get depressed when they tell me I'm the worst person on the planet.

I'm confident because of the things I know I can do. I've worked really hard to become somebody who can climb the highest peaks in the world. I worked really hard to gain entry into one of the most elite units in the British military. I've worked really hard to become a successful author and broadcaster.

There's one other thing you should know about confidence: you won't become confident overnight. You probably won't become confident in a matter of weeks. That's OK! In fact, if you try to bite off the whole thing at once, you might find it's too big to swallow. **You build confidence by taking little steps. Over time, these will add up to a big leap.**

> *Think about something that you really want to try, but that you're a bit nervous about doing. Write that activity down, and also all the reasons why you feel nervous about doing it.*

Lots of things feel intimidating when you think about trying them for the first time. When I first considered climbing Everest, I was really excited, but I was also quite overwhelmed. I knew that it would be one of the most demanding, frightening challenges I had ever taken on.

It is totally normal to feel that anxiety. You might really want to do something, but also be a bit afraid that you might not like it, or won't be very good at it. Perhaps you have always been keen to learn how to code, but are worried that it will be too hard. Or maybe you want to become good at skateboarding, but are scared you'll fall off and look silly.

That's where taking slow, steady steps comes in. If I'd have walked out of my front door in my shorts and tried to climb Everest without having practised or prepared in any way it would have been a disaster. In fact, it would have been such a disaster that I would probably have been put off the idea of climbing mountains for ever. Or, even worse, I might have died and you wouldn't be reading this book right now.

Instead, I broke the whole process into bite-sized bits. I started off by doing lots of research into Everest and the best way to get to its top. Then I contacted people who I knew would have the expertise I lacked, and who would be able to help me on my quest. I trained and trained and trained, working on my physical fitness and my mountain-climbing technique. After that, I did practice climbs of three other, smaller mountains. Every small step I took made me feel more comfortable and confident. As I gained strength, skill and knowledge, the big mission of climbing Mount Everest began to feel less and less intimidating. By the time I had reached base camp, I was sure I'd be able to reach the summit.

And that's what you can do. You identify the big mission (whatever new thing you want to learn), and then the small missions that will help you achieve it. Let's say the big mission is learning how to play tennis.

The first small mission is learning the rules.

Then you might want to get used to holding the tennis racket and the way the ball bounces.

Then you start learning how to hit the ball.

Gradually you will build up your skills. When you approach things step by step, you can actually see your progress. Each mission completed is another accomplishment. And as your skills grow, so too will your confidence. Because you'll have shown yourself exactly what you're capable of.

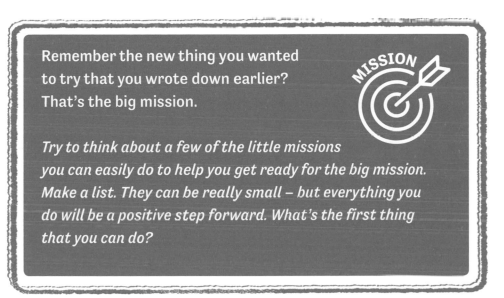

Remember the new thing you wanted to try that you wrote down earlier? That's the big mission.

Try to think about a few of the little missions you can easily do to help you get ready for the big mission. Make a list. They can be really small – but everything you do will be a positive step forward. What's the first thing that you can do?

You probably won't get stuff perfect first time round, but the next time you try it, you'll find it a bit easier. The time after that you'll probably find it even easier! And it's that progress that's so important. Nobody will ever be perfect at what they do. **You're not in competition with anybody else.** Your confidence in yourself shouldn't rest on other people's opinions or their perception of success and failure – what's important is making small, meaningful steps in the right direction. It doesn't matter that you're not Emma Raducanu.

If you enjoy tennis and feel as if you're steadily improving your skills, that's enough. You don't have to be the best in the world. Actually, you don't even need to be the best in your class. **Your only aim should be to get a little bit better today than you were yesterday.** So it doesn't matter if your friend seems have been born with a beautiful singing voice and you can only just hold a tune. If you enjoy it and want to put the effort into improving, then go for it! **Every little bit of progress you make can help boost your confidence.**

Think about Marcus Rashford. He scored in his first games for Manchester United and England. To anybody on the outside, it could have looked as if he found it all easy. He was just a really gifted teenager. But what lay behind all of that was years and years of dedication and practice. He was born talented, but what ensured that he went from being a tiny kid from Wythenshawe to one of the best footballers in the country was the work he put in. He will have practised over and again. He and the people around him (like his mum taking him to training day after day after day) will have sacrificed so much.

Never think you need to rush. Good things often take time. If you've built that confidence up slowly and patiently, it will be much more solid. Think of it like constructing a big wall. If you just rush to put it up in ten minutes, it will look sloppy and will probably collapse the second there's a gust of air.

But if you've put it together carefully, brick by brick, then it will stand up to pretty much anything. You can trust it.

Once you've proved to yourself that you can learn one thing, you'll find that you are more confident about trying lots of other things. If you've learned how to play tennis, why shouldn't you be able to learn how to play the guitar too? Just make sure that it's a skill you want to do for yourself, not something you're trying to pick up to impress others.

If you can steadily build your confidence in this way, you'll feel a change inside. When something new comes along you'll be less afraid of tackling it. And that will translate into a more general sense of confidence. You'll feel more sure of your thoughts and more able to listen to your instincts, because you've shown (to yourself and everybody around you) that you're the sort of person who can do stuff, even when it seems hard or complicated. And you can draw on that inner confidence whenever you have those moments (which we all have) of doubting yourself.

When I was a soldier and I got anxious, I'd take a moment to remind myself of all the stages I'd had to get through to be where I was. All the tests I'd passed, the challenges I'd overcome. It wasn't a question of being big-headed, it was just about being honest. And it really helped. I had earned the right to be there.

It's too easy to focus on what you can't do. What we don't do enough of is record and celebrate the things we can do.

When you're learning something new, why not keep a record of it. You could put it up in your bedroom, or on the fridge door. And if you can't think of something yourself, why not ask a teacher or parent for suggestions. Remember, other people are sometimes better at spotting your progress than you are!

MAKE A LIST OF . . .

- Things I've learned this week
- Things I can do now that I couldn't last week

TIP FOR CHOOSING A NEW SKILL TO LEARN

When you're choosing what new skill to learn, the most important thing to think about isn't whether you're going to go on to be as talented a singer as Taylor Swift, or as good at rugby as Maro Itoje.

What you should look for is something you ENJOY.

If you enjoy something you're much more likely to want to invest the effort needed to get better. When you find something fun and stimulating, you'll be happy to work hard. You probably won't even see it as work! And the more you put into something, the greater its rewards will be.

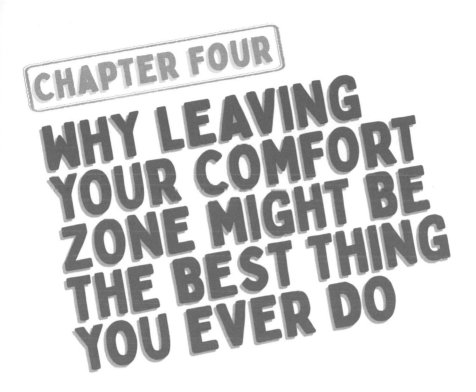

CHAPTER FOUR

WHY LEAVING YOUR COMFORT ZONE MIGHT BE THE BEST THING YOU EVER DO

Everybody likes staying in their comfort zone, don't they? It's safer and easier there. You just do the things you already like and know you're good at. What's wrong with that?

Well, don't get me started! Are you sure you don't want to meet new friends, go to new places, try new things? Staying in your comfort zone might be less frightening, but it will end up being really flipping boring. It's like always playing computer games on the easiest setting. It's good for a bit, but then don't you start to miss the challenge that comes with being tested?

IF YOU WANT TO **GROW** AND LEARN YOU HAVE TO **STRETCH** YOURSELF, AND DO THINGS THAT MIGHT SEEM **DIFFICULT** OR EVEN SCARY.

YOU HAVE TO STEP OUTSIDE YOUR COMFORT ZONE.

But in doing that, you're also taking a step towards brilliant, exciting things.

I'll prove it to you.

Think of all the stuff you like most. Now consider the first time you tried them. Maybe it was joining a local theatre club. Do you remember how nervous you were at that first rehearsal, how anxious meeting new people made you feel, how unsure you were about whether you were brave enough to stand up on stage?

And how about now? If you'd listened to your nerves, you wouldn't have this fantastic thing you can do every Saturday morning. And you wouldn't have got better and better and better at acting.

Human beings are innovators, inventors and explorers. The history of humankind is the history of amazing adventures and incredible discoveries: determined figures trudging through snow, ice, wind and darkness to find the North Pole; the physicist and chemist Marie Curie discovering new elements that made an incalculable difference to our scientific understanding. What's driven all of that is people who've been willing to push themselves a little bit further, a little bit harder, than they had the day before. And do you know what the best thing is? You can do that too! (Although you don't have to get cold or even put on a lab coat . . . unless you want to.)

Taking people out of their comfort zones was an important part of my TV show. We'd never put our contestants in danger, and we'd never ask them to do something that was impossible, but we do make them do stuff they didn't think they were capable of, like jumping out of helicopters into big freezing lakes. Lots of them will sit in the helicopter on the way to the lake saying, 'I can't do it, I can't do it.' Then they leap out into the water (with a bit of encouragement from me) and find that, actually, they flipping well can. They go from being afraid of something to being filled with a bit more confidence.

I try to do something similar in my normal life.

EVERY DAY I ATTEMPT TO DO SOMETHING THAT TAKES ME OUT OF MY COMFORT ZONE.

I WANT TO GIVE MYSELF AS MANY CHANCES AS I CAN TO EXPERIENCE DIFFERENT SITUATIONS, OR PICK UP NEW SKILLS, OR LEARN THINGS ABOUT MYSELF.

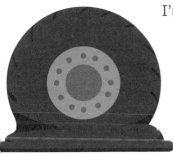

I'm not any kind of mechanic (the idea of DIY brings me out in a sweat), but if I'm driving in my car and I get a puncture, you'd better believe I'm going to try to fix it myself rather than calling a mechanic to come and help. It might take two hours, my hands might end up raw and dirty, I might get so angry that I go red and shout a lot, but I'll have stretched myself and learned something new.

I do the same when there's a delay on the train I'm on. Instead of waiting in the station I'll jump out. I'll find a bus or take a taxi. Anything to test myself and make my brain work. It gives me practice at solving problems and of coping in unfamiliar environments.

It's probably best that you don't do exactly what I do, but you can do stuff to get a similar effect. And just like when it comes to learning a new skill, you should take it gradually. You don't need to be jumping into pits of cobras, or wrestling bears. What I'm talking about is those activities or situations that are just on the edge of what you find comfortable. Perhaps you could put your hand up to answer a question in class, even if you're not absolutely sure of the answer. Or you might be in the school lunch queue and see a small kid being pushed by an older student. Normally you might just ignore it and pretend it isn't happening. But why not step out of your comfort zone by being kind and standing up for the kid being pushed?

Do only as much as you can bear. Next time you'll be able to go that tiny bit further. You just need to be stretching and challenging yourself. Remember when I said that the brain was a bit like a muscle? The more you push it, the stronger it gets!

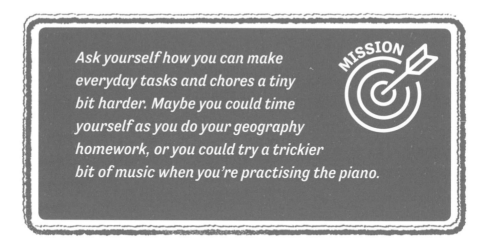

Ask yourself how you can make everyday tasks and chores a tiny bit harder. Maybe you could time yourself as you do your geography homework, or you could try a trickier bit of music when you're practising the piano.

The more experience of dealing with these demanding, complex situations you give yourself, the tougher and nimbler your brain will be, and the better you'll be able to cope when something bigger and more frightening arrives.

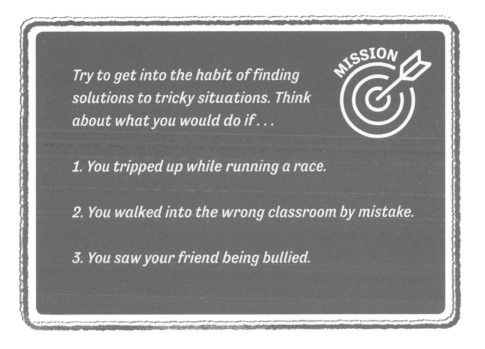

Try to get into the habit of finding solutions to tricky situations. Think about what you would do if . . .

1. You tripped up while running a race.

2. You walked into the wrong classroom by mistake.

3. You saw your friend being bullied.

'Aha!' you might say, 'but what happens if stepping out of my comfort zone is so tough it just makes me want to give up?' My answer would be: 'Anybody who claims they've never wanted to throw in the towel is a BIG FAT LIAR. But that doesn't mean you have to quit.'

There's a lot of power in perseverance. It's what keeps you going when you've stepped out of your comfort zone and all you really want to do is step back into it again. It's what keeps you going when there's that little voice in your head saying, 'Give up, give up!'

I've already told you about some of the extreme adventures I've been on, whether that's climbing mountains, or trying to make my way across an ocean in a fragile wooden boat. What I haven't told you, is that they all have one thing in common: at some point, I wanted to quit.

There's always a morning when you wake up feeling exhausted. And that tiredness might be made worse by bad weather (hailstones that rain down on you like bullets, a sun so hot it feels as if it's stripping the skin from your face or wind that seems like it's doing its best to steal your clothes!).

Then there's pain. I remember how on one expedition the day had begun badly before we'd even set off. Just as dawn broke, a storm began. Torrential rain. Vicious winds. Things got even worse when, an hour in, the pain started. I felt it first in my legs, then up through my torso and then into my arms. Everything became one dull ache. Then I slipped and twisted my ankle. FLIP! Every step I took afterwards sent a shot of agony up my leg. I began to worry that I wouldn't be able to go on. I could feel the temptation to just give up pulling at me.

What helped me get through the pain barrier and drag myself on were two thoughts. As I trudged on and on, with rain beating down on me and the wind lashing my face, I kept on telling myself how amazing it would feel if I managed to finish my journey without having to call for help. I'd be achieving something I'd dreamed of for years, and had spent months planning. I imagined the pride on my family's faces. That gave me a boost when I needed it most. What also helped inspire me to carry on was considering the consequences of abandoning the expedition. I thought about how disappointed I'd be with myself if I chucked the whole thing in. It would have been such a waste of my blood, sweat and tears. I couldn't do that to myself. So I carried on, one excruciating step after another.

There's no shame in finding something difficult. That just means you're stretching yourself. You're becoming a better version of you! But if you're trying something new and you feel your will to carry on ebbing away, try to do these two things:

1. Think about how good it would feel if you didn't give up.

2. Think about how disappointing it would be if you did give up. Maybe there have already been times when you've been doing something hard and considering giving up, but carried on. How did that make you feel?

I've learned to love feedback. So can you! It's easy to get upset when someone points out that you've messed up, or got something a bit wrong, especially when you have stepped out of your comfort zone to try something new. I remember how embarrassed and upset I would feel when I was at school and the teacher handed my work back to me covered in corrections. I convinced myself they were picking on me. Every part of me was screaming: 'This isn't fair!'

But it's possible to take a different perspective. Maybe instead of complaining, you should consider embracing those times when another person shows you how you could something differently?

The first thing to remember when you receive constructive criticism is that **everybody messes up sometimes.** It may upset you, especially if you have tried hard and put lots of effort into something, but try and remember that the person who corrected you is probably just trying to help. They're not trying to make you feel silly. In fact it's probably the opposite: they care about you and don't want you to make the same mistake twice.

Take a moment to think about the last occasion you got feedback. Maybe it was a teacher showing you where you went wrong in a maths test, or a basketball coach showing you a better way of dribbling. It's always nice to be told that you're brilliant and doing everything really well. But praise doesn't teach you anything. How would you ever learn to complete that maths problem, or improve your dribbling, if you didn't get feedback? If the criticism is designed to help you do better next time, by giving you a clear sense of what you could do differently, then it's always worth listening to.

Instead of seeing feedback as somebody pushing you down, you should see it for what it really is: that person is giving you a hand up.

And yet, here's the big BUT (and yes, I know it sounds like I've just said something rude). I've been around the block long enough to know that not all feedback is positive. Occasionally somebody will tell you that you're rubbish, but they don't bother to tell you how you could improve. That's negative criticism. The only thing it achieves is making you feel bad. And sometimes people will be critical of you not because they're trying to help, but because they're jealous, or insecure, or just plain mean.

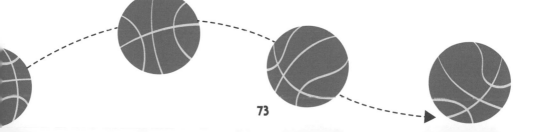

73

If somebody is saying stuff that's designed to bring you down rather than lift you up, the best thing you can do is ignore it. They're a negative person trying to pass their negativity on to you. It isn't about you, it's about their own unhappiness, so there's absolutely no need for you to even listen to it.

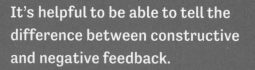

It's helpful to be able to tell the difference between constructive and negative feedback.

Read the two examples below, then think about the ways in which they're different.

'Jack, I liked your enthusiasm there. Just try to listen right to the end of the instruction before getting up to do the task. Otherwise you might miss something you need to know.'

'Jack, you got that all wrong. You've got to do better next time.'

Which comment is helpful and which is unhelpful and not constructive? How would you feel if a teacher said them to you?

BULLIES

Sometimes it can feel as if bullies were put on the planet to take us out of our comfort zone. I've met a fair few in my time. And, do you know what? Mostly, I feel sorry for them. Bullies are attention-seekers. They act up because they're angry and insecure. It's almost never personal – they just want to make somebody else feel as bad as they do. The big thing I've realised is that nothing good ever came from interacting with a bully. If you can, steer well clear of them. Put as much physical space between them and yourself as possible. If I can, I'll always try to be smarter than the situation and stay away from encounters that I know could make me feel uncomfortable, or that might even escalate into something worse. (If there's one thing I've learned from being in the military, it's that putting yourself in unnecessary danger is a terrible idea.) But if avoiding the bullies becomes impossible, there are always things you can do.

TIPS FOR DEALING WITH BULLIES

1. Tell somebody. You don't have to face this alone. Speak to an adult – it could be a parent, or teacher, or any grown-up you trust. They might not be able to make the situation better immediately, but just talking about it will make you feel less alone.

2. If you can't stay out of the bully's way, then try to make sure you're never alone with them. Perhaps you could ask a friend to act as your 'buddy' on the bus, or on the walk home from school.

3. Don't react. Bullies feed off the responses they get from other people. Keep your face as neutral and free from emotion as you can. Show them that you don't care by acting as if you're not interested in what they're saying. Maybe you could start texting on your phone. (For a tip on how to control your emotions, turn to page 115.)

4. If you end up in a confrontation, do everything you can to avoid being aggressive. This is what they want! Instead, tell them firmly that you want them to stop, then walk away.

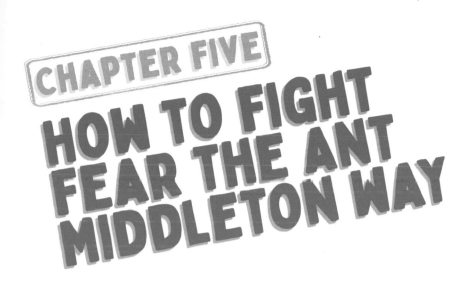

CHAPTER FIVE

HOW TO FIGHT FEAR THE ANT MIDDLETON WAY

I have a reputation for being fearless. People think that because I've been in the Marines and the Special Forces and sailed around the Pacific in a leaky wooden canoe that I somehow never get scared.

But that's not true. Actually, it couldn't be further from the truth. I feel fear all the time. I get nervous before I speak in public, I get nervous before I start filming a new programme, I get terrified in small spaces. You get the picture . . .

And I know I'm not alone.

EVERYONE FEELS FRIGHTENED SOMETIMES.

And if they claim they haven't, then they're a big flipping liar. I was in the military with some of the toughest people in the country. We'd been all round the world. We'd seen all sorts of things. We'd been trained to be the absolute best we could be at what we did. But I know for a fact that every single person I served alongside will have been scared or nervous at some point.

So I'm not alone when I say that I often feel afraid. And I bet I'm not the only one who hates it when fear strikes. It makes me feel vulnerable and small. I want to curl up and hide away. That was true when I was a kid and is still true now. The difference is that over the years I've learned how to use that fear and control it. **AND YOU CAN DO THE SAME.**

The most important thing to understand is that you'll never become totally fearless. You can't flush fear down the toilet or throw it into your neighbour's garden. You can't hide it away in your friend's schoolbag and hope they'll take it home with them. Like any emotion, it's a part of who we are as human beings. Fear is absolutely natural. There's no shame in feeling afraid. For thousands of years it has been an essential part of humankind's survival. Our bodies were designed that way!

TIP FOR UNDERSTANDING YOUR FEAR

When it intrudes into normal life, fear can be really annoying, even upsetting. Nobody enjoys feeling anxious before giving a presentation. Most of this chapter is about learning how to control or redirect that sort of fear. But there are times when it can be REALLY useful and the best thing you can do is listen to it. If, for example, you heard a loud sound behind you, your body would get a surge of adrenaline and jump to alert you to potential danger, so don't ignore it! You should trust the messages your body is sending you. It knows when you're in a situation that could be dangerous.

But so many of us feel powerless when fear strikes.
It paralyses us, it can sit on our shoulders, weighing us
down until we feel as if we can barely breathe. *Uncontrolled*
fear is what stops us from becoming the best version of
ourselves. It means we don't go out and try things, meet
people, or visit places that could make us happier and
enrich our lives.

The second most important thing to understand is that you
CAN control it. Once you realise that, you can also start to
make it work for you. Neat, isn't it?

Then you'll find it becomes a lot easier to take those steps
outside your comfort zone that are so crucial to learning
and growing. You'll be able to use those nerves that run
up and down your spine before you go into an exam to help
you perform even better. You'll even be able to tackle those
nagging terrors that keep you awake at night.

*Make a list of three things that you'd
like to do but are afraid to try. What
is it that makes you nervous?*

THE FEELING

I bet you know **The Feeling**. It comes in the minutes before
you have to read aloud in class. Or in the hours before
you're about to sing in public. Sometimes it even happens
when you're preparing to go back to school on a Monday.
You feel hot all over. Your stomach seems to be doing
backflips. When you try to speak, your voice is all stumbly –
you can't be sure if you're making sense.

Anxiety, fear, nerves. You can call it what you want.
The Feeling is the product of the adrenaline our body
makes when it thinks it's faced with a threat (it doesn't
care if that's an exam or a sabre-toothed tiger or a bunch
of nine-legged aliens that have just landed from outer
space). Adrenaline makes our hearts beat faster and our
breathing quicker. It even makes us sweat.

All of that can feel overwhelming. Often we get into such a state that we aren't able to perform as well as we know we can.

That's probably why we have all learned to see **The Feeling** as negative. It's a curse that can only be endured. Some days it will be really bad, at other times less so, but there's not much you can do about it.

Except that maybe there is . . . Here's another way of looking at **The Feeling**. What if I told you that the adrenaline is just your body's way of saying:

The butterflies in your tummy, the wobbliness when you speak — it's a preparation! It's a sign that whatever you're about to do matters to you, and that your limbs, your brain, your lungs and your heart are keen to play their part and help out.

Let's take the minutes before you're due to give a presentation in class as an example. First, imagine how you might feel if you saw those nerves as purely negative.

Q. 'What's this feeling that is making me feel panicked and sweaty?'

A. 'Hmmm, is it fear?'

Q. 'What thoughts are going through your head?'

A. 'I can't do this, it's too hard. I'm going to make a fool of myself.'

Q. 'What impact is this having on your behaviour?'

A. 'Er, I feel like I'm frozen to the spot. Every cell in my body is telling me to HIDE UNDER THE TABLE.'

Now, what about if you saw the nerves as positive?

Q. 'What's this feeling that is making me feel panicked and sweaty?'

A. 'Yep, it's still fear.'

Q. 'What thoughts are going through your head?'

A. 'Wow, look at all this adrenaline pumping through my body. I CAN do this. I just have to give it a go.'

Q. 'What impact is this having on your behaviour?'

A. 'I'm calm, I feel in control. It's like my body's working with me, not against me.'

This is a really simple technique that people who are a lot cleverer than me would call re-framing. **If you can change the way you look at something, then you can change the way it affects you.** Instead of seeing all that adrenaline as your body trying to trip you up, try to look at it as your body giving you a boost. Because if you can start to see fear as an ally rather than an enemy, you'll find that instead of making you feel jittery or paralysed, all the adrenaline running through your body will become an amazing source of energy. You can use it to focus your mind, or push your legs to run that bit faster. It's like suddenly finding you're attached to a rocket.

MISSION

Let's draw a body map! Spend a couple of minutes thinking about how being anxious or afraid makes all the different parts of your body feel. Then write them all down.

For example, you could write something like this:

Stomach: tingly
Legs: jiggly
Mouth: dry

THE FEAR BUBBLE

When I was a soldier, there were times when I almost felt crippled by my fear of the things that lay in the future. It used to sit heavily in my stomach. It made me feel nauseous and angry with myself. 'This is my dream job,' I'd tell myself, 'so why am I so unhappy and afraid all the time?' It really troubled me, and this disquiet lasted until I started to ask myself some questions.

I started to think hard about WHY I was feeling scared, and WHEN.

Why was I afraid two weeks before I'd even set off for Afghanistan, when I was still in the safety of my family home? Why was I afraid in a military base that was guarded by many hundreds of other soldiers? I was more in danger there from a stubbed toe than I was from enemy bullets.

Whatever you do in life, the bit you actually fear – the **fear bubble**, as I came to call it – only lasts a short amount of time. An interview or an exam rarely lasts much more than an hour, often they're only a few minutes. But somehow that fear infects the hours, days and weeks that lead up to it. It drains people and stops them from enjoying other aspects of their lives.

The problem is that obsessing about the challenge you're facing isn't going to make it go away. In fact, the more you think about it, the worse it gets.

The solution, I decided, was to try to look at the situation more rationally. I realised that it was irrational to feel fear at any other point than when I was inside the fear bubble.

This allowed me to break the fear down into smaller, more digestible chunks. I stopped seeing fear as a powerful, all-consuming force that was around me every minute of the day. Instead I tried to treat it as a specific place and time that I wouldn't worry about until I needed to step into it.

Do everything you need to make sure you're as ready as you can be, but don't waste time or energy worrying about something that isn't affecting you at that precise moment. If you've done the preparation you need to, why should you be nervous a whole week or even day beforehand?

So, if you've got an exam coming up, think of it as existing in its own bubble. The only time you need to be in that bubble is when you're actually in the classroom and you've got the paper sitting in front of you. You don't need to enter that bubble when you're at home in the days leading up to the exam, or when you're lying in bed the night before, or even on the bus on the way into school on the morning of the exam itself. Give it a go!

TIP FOR DEALING WITH NERVOUS ENERGY

A lot of the time our fears are fed by nervous energy. Our whole body feels as if it's been flooded with adrenaline, and maybe one leg begins to jog up and down, as if it has a life of its own. And then our anxiety begins to spiral. It's your body telling you something! Whenever that happens to me, I find the best thing to do is to divert that nervous energy into a positive direction. Instead of sitting down and letting my mind fill with worries, I'll go to the gym. Afterwards I'll always feel calmer. You could achieve the same by taking the dog for a walk, or getting your skipping rope out for ten minutes, or turning cartwheels. Whatever helps you to work that nervous energy out of your system.

THE PROCESS

Of course, not all of our fears are of specific events, like tests or visiting a relative in hospital. Sometimes we simply feel anxious without being able to explain why. This can feel overwhelminq.

There's a myth that it's possible to remove these sorts of fears in the same way that you might rip off a plaster: a sharp bit of pain and then it's all over. I think this is just not true.

YOU ROB A FEAR OF THE POWER IT HAS OVER YOU IN EXACTLY THE SAME WAY AS YOU CAN BUILD YOUR CONFIDENCE.

TAKE IT SLOWLY, EXPOSE YOURSELF TO IT A LITTLE AT A TIME.

Imagine that you're afraid of heights. Just the idea of being in a tall building is enough to make your stomach churn and your head start spinning. You could try and resolve that problem by going straight up a swimming pool's highest diving board and then leaping off it into the water below. That could work, but it's more likely that you'll end up feeling so overwhelmed with fear that you won't ever want to even go up a ladder again. You'll have bitten off much more than you can chew.

It's much better to take a slow and steady approach. Perhaps you could take diving lessons – having somebody experienced to talk you through the process can really help. Then, when your confidence has grown, you could go a little bit further up the ladder each time you visit the pool. Step just outside your comfort zone. Look around you, think about how you feel, then go back down. Don't feel the need to force anything. There's no rush. It doesn't matter if it takes a year or more to conquer that fear. When you feel ready, try the lowest diving board. Then think about giving the next board up a go. Every tiny bit higher you go is another bite you've taken out of that fear.

Think about a fear you have currently. Write down how you could gradually reduce the power it has over you. (Make sure you include little rewards along the way so that you can celebrate how far you've come!) Try to imagine how strong and confident you'll feel once you've finally conquered that anxiety. For instance, if you're worried about performing in public, take a deep breath and visualise stepping onto the stage. You've practised hard, you've learned your lines and you feel confident. So confident, in fact, that you give everyone a big smile!

How does this exercise make you feel?

THE ONE THING YOU SHOULD NEVER BE AFRAID OF

You should never be afraid of what other people think about you. Never in a million years. No matter what they say, no matter how loudly they say it, no matter who they say it to. As long as you're not being cruel, as long as your intentions are good, then you shouldn't ever be scared about anybody else's opinion. If you like that jumper, then wear it! If you like that song, then sing it!

Actually, there's one other thing you should never be afraid of . . . failure. And that's what we're going to be talking about in the next chapter.

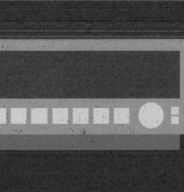

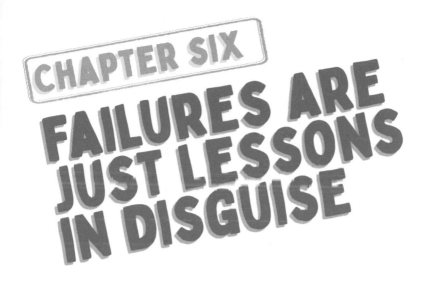

CHAPTER SIX
FAILURES ARE JUST LESSONS IN DISGUISE

A few years ago, I was sent to prison. It was a horrible failure, one of the worst experiences of my life. And yet the lessons I learned from getting through it all, and facing up to the consequences of my actions, helped turn my time behind bars into one of the best things that could have happened to me. I wouldn't be as resilient as I am now if I hadn't gone to prison. Let me explain what I mean by that. And I'm not saying you need to go to prison to learn this!

For a while after leaving the military I hung out with a bad crowd. We all got into too many fights. I got involved in things I should have stayed well clear of.

One night, I got angry and made a terrible, inexcusable mistake that ended with me striking a police officer. My own stupid actions led to me being sentenced to fourteen months in prison. It meant that not only was I separated from my family, but there was also nothing I could do to help or support them.

I remember being in the cramped little van that took me from the court to Chelmsford prison. There was a moment when I almost thought I would be suffocated by the shame I felt. I had gone from being a respected member of an elite fighting unit and a loving family man, to a prisoner sleeping on a thin, ragged mattress in a lonely cell.

In the first days after I'd heard the horrible clang as the door of my cell shut, I wished more than anything that something, or someone, would come along and fix everything for me. It was bewildering, awful. But then I realised that what had happened couldn't be changed or undone. I would have to accept that I'd made a serious mistake and do what I could to move on. I knew that no matter how much I might want to blame others for the part they had played in events that had led me here, that wouldn't help much either. I was here because of what I had done.

Taking responsibility like that was so important, because it helped me see the lessons I needed to learn if I was to avoid finding myself in a situation like this again. I knew that when I was released I was going to have to make a lot of changes. I couldn't be around the same people any more, I had to find a way of controlling my temper, and I had to remember who the most important human beings in my life were (my wife and kids, of course!).

I also realised that I couldn't dwell on the mistake or let it define me. Yes, I made a big, flipping mess, and I'd never deny that, but once I'd extracted those lessons, I had to put prison behind me. There was no use in obsessing over it. I wanted people to remember my response to the mistake more vividly than the mistake itself.

NOBODY IS PERFECT. NOBODY. NOT A SINGLE PERSON.

Everyone makes mistakes. Your parents do, politicians do. Everyone. It's OK to lose, it's OK to trip up and stumble. Everybody does it. It's part of life.

So if you've had a setback, make sure you remind yourself that you're not the first person to fail, and you certainly won't be the last. If you don't believe me, then maybe looking at this list of famous 'failures' will help change your mind.

Walt Disney (the guy who founded the company that made films like *Aladdin, The Little Mermaid, The Lion King* and *Pirates of the Caribbean*) was sacked as a journalist because his editor thought that he 'lacked imagination and had no good ideas'. Apparently for a while he was so poor that he had to eat dog food. (YUCK!)

Twelve different publishers rejected the manuscript of Harry Potter by J.K. Rowling.

Michael Jordan, probably the best basketball player of all time, couldn't even get into his own high school basketball team.

I could fill up this book with other examples, but I think you'd agree that could get a tiny bit boring. The point is that, although they're all really different people from different walks of life, they all had one thing in common: none of them gave up. They hung on in there. They all found ways of bouncing back from their failures. And these setbacks actually became the foundation of their later successes.

HOW TO RESPOND TO A FAILURE

The first thing to remember is that no matter how agonising the setback feels as it's unfolding, you will survive it. Remember what I said in an earlier chapter about how you're stronger than you think? Well, that's a million per cent the case here. **You will get over the pain, and you will bounce back.** I thought that going to prison would break me into pieces, but it didn't.

NO FAILURE IS EVER FINAL,

THERE'S ALWAYS A WAY BACK.

And failures never matter as much as we tell ourselves that they do. If you trip over a couple of words when you're reading in class, does it really matter? Will anybody else care? Will they even notice? No, of course not!

But what you can't do is go back in time and change the result. You can't alter the answers in the exam you failed. You can't stop yourself tripping over during that race. So don't dwell on it. What's happened to you is just one small event in a lifetime full of thousands of events. You'll get plenty of other chances.

TIP FOR DEALING WITH MISTAKES

I know how hard it is to stop reliving mistakes. They cycle round and round in your head, driving you mad. What helps me is reminding myself that whatever the mistake is, it doesn't define me as a person. Winning feels better than losing, of course. But the most important thing isn't coming home with a medal, it's that you tried your best. As long as I can look back and know that I've given everything I could, there's no defeat, no error I can make that bothers me too much.

If the bad news is that you can't change the past, then the good news is that you can do something about the future.
Nice! Your first task is to take responsibility for what happened. It might be tempting to blame everybody but yourself, but you're robbing yourself of the chance to learn a lesson. If you failed that test because you didn't revise, that's on you.

Your second task is to take a bit of time to sit down and think about what went wrong. Once you've done this, you can start planning to make sure that next time you won't make the same mistake again. Maybe you said something hurtful to one of your friends and they got upset. Rather than blame them for being too sensitive, why not calmly ask them how your words made them feel. Try to look at the situation from their perspective. You might still see things differently to them, but it's important to think carefully about what you said, and how you can avoid making them feel bad next time you speak to them. Embrace the chance you've been given to start again with a clean slate.

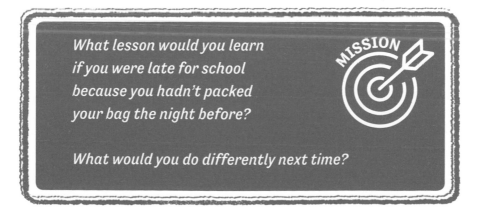

What lesson would you learn if you were late for school because you hadn't packed your bag the night before?

What would you do differently next time?

Going to prison is just one of my failures. I reckon I've already made a million mistakes in my life. I make new ones every day. I'll probably make a million more before I die. And that's fine, because each one has played its part in making me the human being I am now. I'm not afraid of failure, because I know that it's the best education there is. Nothing helps you grow like being knocked down. It pushes your brain into overload. You don't learn anything new when you win. You get handed a whole flipping lot of lessons when you lose.

And just like me, you can reframe the way you view failure. Instead of being afraid of it, and letting that fear hold us back from doing cool, fun stuff that might otherwise make us happy, we should embrace it. It's not just that failures teach us lessons; very often they're actually stepping stones on the way to success. In fact, I reckon that **failure is actually an essential part of success**. I've always said that if you don't make mistakes, you don't make anything. If you don't open yourself up to the chance of failure, you'll end up stagnating. You won't get to learn and grow.

Before I summited Everest, I failed to reach three far smaller peaks. But I don't see these as failures. I wouldn't have been able to get to the top of Everest without my experiences on the Matterhorn and Aconcagua and Elbrus. Every failure allowed me to gain more experience and learn new lessons. More importantly, although I didn't reach their summits, each time I failed to summit the smaller peak, I was still managing to climb higher than I ever had before. What some people might call failure, I saw as progress.

It took Thomas Edison, who was one of the most incredible inventors of all time, more than 10,000 attempts to create a lightbulb that he could sell to a mass audience. He knew that failures aren't steps back. They are very often steps forward. As he said,

'I have <u>NOT</u> failed 10,000 times.
I have <u>NOT</u> failed once.

I have SUCCEEDED in proving that those 10,000 ways will not work.

When I have eliminated the ways that will not work, I will find the way that <u>WILL</u> work.'

He didn't see what he did as failing. He saw it as an exercise in problem-solving. And every time he got something wrong, it brought him closer to his destination.

Another thing people overlook is that very often what look like failures to begin with are actually opportunities to grow! We can get so caught up in certain ways of doing things, and certain ways of thinking, that we don't realise that we're in a bit of a rut. The failure might seem shocking while it's unfolding, but when stuff gets smashed to pieces it allows us to see the world in a different way and gives us the chance to put everything back together again in new, better ways. It allows us to evolve and develop in important ways.

Try to think of three times in your life, or the lives of your family and friends, when stuff that initially seemed like a failure actually ended up becoming an opportunity.

MISSION

I was in a rut before I got arrested. I'd left the Army and was working as a bodyguard. It wasn't something I liked very much (it was super boring), but I couldn't see a way of finding a job I did like, and I was mixing with people who were bad news. I wouldn't have realised this if I hadn't gone to prison. It was only because of the changes I made to the way I lived after I was released that exciting opportunities, like going on telly, fell into my path. I wouldn't have become a television star – and you wouldn't be reading this book right now – if I hadn't failed in such a big way.

WHAT I THOUGHT AT THE TIME WAS THE LOWEST POINT OF MY LIFE . . .

ENDED UP BEING THE THING THAT HELPED TURN IT AROUND.

So go out bravely into the world. Try new things. And never let the fear of failure hold you back. When you trip up (and you will trip up, I promise you), just pick yourself up, dust yourself down and go again. Next time you'll be stronger, you'll know more, you'll be better prepared.

YOU'LL SMASH IT!!!

But before you turn to the next section, why don't we put what you've learned about failure into practice? I'm going to give you two situations on page 109 where I made a bit of a mess of things. And don't worry, if you need to refresh your memory about the tips I've given you, it's OK to flick back through the chapter! I've included what I ended up doing on pages 110–11. I wonder how similar our answers will be!

What would you do to respond to these failures if you were in my shoes? Is there anything there that you could transform into an opportunity?

Q1. A friend let me down by not turning up for something when he'd promised he would. Before I'd given the situation any thought I sent him an angry text message. This hurt his feelings and we got into an argument and didn't speak to each other for a bit. (Don't worry, we're pals again now!)

Q2. When I was a young soldier I wanted to test myself by joining the elite Parachute Regiment. The problem was that I kept struggling during the endurance test that was part of the selection process. We had to do these really long runs carrying rucksacks that were full of weights. It was hard for me because my legs were a bit shorter than all the other recruits'. Every time we went on one of these runs, I came last. It really felt to me as if I was failing. I was at risk of being thrown off the course.

My answer to Q1. The situation with my flaky friend taught me that although sending an angry text message might make you feel better in the short term, it actually can end up causing upset and difficulty in the long term. Instead of firing off an insult in the heat of the moment, I should have given myself time and space to cool down. It took me a while to be able to see things from my friend's perspective. But once I had put myself in his shoes, I realised that I had over-reacted. Behaving aggressively only leads to more trouble. If you've got a problem with somebody, it's far better to raise your concerns in a calm, measured manner.

My answer to Q2. My solution to the problem with my legs was simple. I realised that complaining about the physical advantage other people had wouldn't get me anywhere. I'd just be left feeling bitter. If I wanted to get into the Parachute Regiment, then I had to be willing to work twice as hard as anybody else. So that's what I did. I hit the gym hard to build up my muscles. I went on extra runs to build up my fitness. It was really hard going, but it paid off. After a while, I found that I was no longer coming in last, I was actually getting much closer to the front. In time, it was enough to make sure I passed the course.

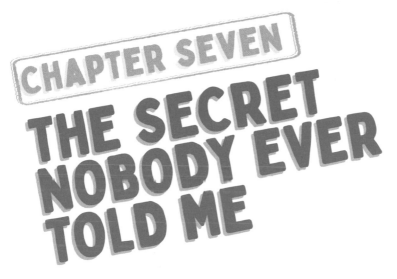

CHAPTER SEVEN

THE SECRET NOBODY EVER TOLD ME

Do you want to know an amazing fact? Often when we're upset, or hurt, or just very happy, we cry (emotions are confusing, right?). But if you looked at those tears under a microscope, you'd see that the sort of emotion you'd been experiencing had determined the structure of the tears you'd just shed. Angry tears look different to sad ones. Ecstatic tears look different to frustrated ones.

We all experience emotions, they're an integral part of being human. There isn't a single person on the planet who hasn't felt rage or sadness or joy so extreme it makes them jump up and down.

WE SHOULDN'T BE ASHAMED OF OUR EMOTIONS: THEY'RE A SIGN THAT WE'RE ALIVE!

The problem is that occasionally these emotions can be overwhelming and we don't always know how to cope with them. Something tragic happens and there's so much sadness inside us that it seems that our heart will burst. Or somebody makes us lose our temper and we do and say a lot of stupid stuff that we regret later.

The thing that nobody told me when I was a kid (and flipping heck, I wished they had), is that **it is possible to control your emotions**. If we can't stop every bad thing happening, what we can do is change how we respond to those uncomfortable or upsetting situations.

This isn't about cutting yourself off from your emotions and becoming a cold, unfeeling robot. What I'm suggesting is the opposite, it's about being as connected to them as you can be.

Before we start on that process, it's important to acknowledge that quite a lot of stuff happens in the world that is out of our hands. That might sound a bit scary, but to me it's amazingly liberating. If I can't control it, I don't need to worry about it. I'm free to focus my attention on the things I can control. You CAN'T stop your mum from being stressed by her job. You CAN'T make it sunny every day. You CAN'T make Arsenal win every week. But you CAN take charge of the things you say, the things you do, and, most importantly, the things you think.

I used to hate going on stage and speaking to crowds of people. I felt so exposed, as if all my vulnerabilities were on show. It made me horribly nervous. I just wasn't used to it, but it was becoming a bigger and bigger part of my job so I had to find a way of coping. I realised that the best way to keep my anxiety at a level I was comfortable with was to concentrate on what I could control and avoid worrying about what I couldn't.

TIP FOR DEALING WITH EMOTIONS

Making a list like this really helped me.

I COULD CONTROL

- Working really hard on a good script
- Arriving at the venue in time to get myself ready properly (I *hate* being in a rush)
- My body language

I COULDN'T CONTROL

- How many people would turn up
- Whether people would laugh at my jokes
- Whether people would even like me

This exercise made a massive difference. I didn't waste energy thinking about stuff I knew I couldn't change, and although I still felt that familiar little prickle of nerves as I was waiting to go on stage, I was no longer afraid that my emotions would overwhelm me.

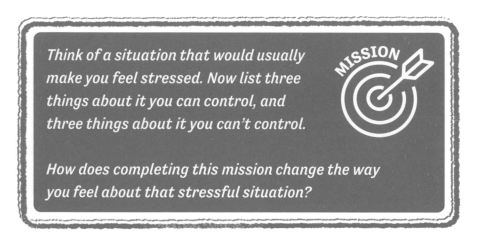

Think of a situation that would usually make you feel stressed. Now list three things about it you can control, and three things about it you can't control.

How does completing this mission change the way you feel about that stressful situation?

What I've just talked about could be seen as the first step towards developing emotional awareness. (I know this sounds a bit complex, but it really isn't – I promise you, if I can do this, you definitely can.) As I see it, **emotional awareness is simply a question of being able to understand any given emotion for what it is, then making it work for you.** Because the moment an emotion isn't working for you, then guess what – it'll start working against you. Nightmare!

It can be unsettling and even scary if you see your emotions as mysterious forces that blow in and out of your life without any explanation. That's why I always encourage people to be curious about their feelings. If you deny that they even exist, you're always going to be at their mercy. You won't know when they're going to come, or how to handle them when they arrive. Instead, you should try to learn as much as you can about them so that they can become familiar, and comprehensible. Break those emotions down into chunks you can easily digest.

PRIDE

EXCITEMENT

HAPPINESS

If I feel a strong emotion, I won't just let it float away. I'll try to grab it, study it. I'll ask myself what exactly it is that I'm feeling.

Then I ask myself why I think all of this is happening.

One of the most physically and psychologically challenging things I've ever done was a show called *Mutiny*. Along with eight volunteers, I recreated a famous 4,000-mile journey from Tonga to Timor made by a group of sailors who'd been chucked off their ship by the rest of the crew. (Doesn't sound like a nice thing to do, does it?) I was determined that we would be as faithful to the original conditions as possible. So we sailed in a replica of their tiny wooden canoe.

We navigated using charts, refused waterproof clothing and struggled on a diet of hard biscuits and water that eventually started to smell of rotten eggs.

It was unbelievably hard. The sun was so hot it melted our camera batteries. What made it even harder was the behaviour of one of the other men on board. He complained about literally everything. He wasn't pulling his weight on the canoe, and whenever we tried to challenge him, he claimed we were picking on him. (Believe me, we weren't.) But I felt I could ignore him. I'd seen worse in my time!

Still, although I had begun the journey full of excitement, halfway through I found myself becoming irritable. I was snapping at everybody else. I could feel tension gripping my chest so tight that it was occasionally hard to breathe, and I struggled to concentrate even on essential tasks. Eventually a moment came when I was about to really shout at one of the other crew members for having made a tiny mistake. What was happening to me? That's when I decided I need to break down what I was feeling.

I knew I was hungry, thirsty and tired. And I missed my wife and kids. But that was the point of the trip. It was supposed to be tough. That's what I'd wanted. Then I realised: it was rage. I was furious at the guy who'd been causing all that trouble. I thought I'd been letting his behaviour wash over me, but actually it was sitting there in my body, causing all sorts of mischief.

Just being able to identify and explain that emotion was incredibly empowering. It was now something I understood, not some inexplicable force swirling through my brain. And now I knew what I was facing, and why, I could start to take steps to start feeling better. If I hadn't recognised what I was experiencing as anger, how could I ever have done anything about it?

Next time you're feeling worried or stressed, why not try this exercise?

Close your eyes and really try to identify what is worrying you. Then acknowledge these worries by naming them out loud. But (and this is the cool bit) as you're speaking, imagine that the worry you've just named is floating away on a cloud.

You don't need to be on a boat in the middle of the Pacific ocean to begin this process. Say, for example, you've been waiting for ages in the queue for lunch at school and an extremely rude kid barges in ahead of you. And as if that isn't bad enough, he snaffles up the bit of the lasagne (the LAST one!!!) that you've had your eye on. All that's left is a weird grey stew that has really some nasty lumps in it. Urgh. Suddenly you feel your body temperature soaring, you really, really want to pick up that pot of stew and throw it over the boy, who is already tucking happily into that delicious lasagne.

Instead of giving in to all those shouty feelings that are running around your body, stop for a second and think.

Q. "What emotion am I feeling?"

A. "Er, anger."

Q. "And why are you feeling it?"

A. "Isn't it obvious? He's got my *LASAGNE*!"

Taking that moment to reflect on what you're feeling and why is crucial. It's a bit like pressing the pause button when you're playing a computer game. Suddenly all the action stops and you can make a calm decision about what you're going to do next. You also get this chance to really take in what's going on around you. You notice things on screen that you won't see when everything is unfolding at a hectic pace. **When you press the pause button in real life, it prevents your emotions racing out of control.** And every time you do it, you'll have learned a bit more about how your emotions work.

Just as with almost everything I've talked about so far, don't worry if you don't get it quite right first time round. Or second time round. Or third time round. Try, fail, try and fail again. Each time you give it a go, you'll be getting more confident and more familiar with your feelings.

After a while, you can be even more detailed in the sorts of questions you ask yourself. If you occasionally get so mad you hop about and scream, try to work out if there are any particular situations that trigger that anger. Maybe you can find ways of avoiding them? But, even if you can't, just knowing that those sorts of situations are triggering can ensure that you go into them better prepared to respond.

The other important step you can take once you've identified that emotion is finding a way of using it to your advantage. You can flip that negative into a positive. Let's return to The Infuriating Case of the Stolen Lasagne. Rather than giving in to temptation and expressing the anger you feel by soaking your new enemy from head to toe in grey stew, why not use that rage for something productive. Perhaps you can draw on it to give you energy during your P.E. lesson that afternoon? Or it could be the thing that helps you focus when you're trying to pull off a complex trick on your BMX.

TIPS FOR DEALING WITH STRESSFUL SITUATIONS

When everything feels as if it's getting a bit too much for you, why not try the following?

1. Close your eyes and count to ten.

2. Take deep, slow breaths (you'll feel calmer very quickly – I promise!).

3. Go for a walk or a run – being outside in the fresh air really helps.

4. Do something that absorbs you, like a puzzle or drawing a picture.

5. Play with a pet (no, really, it's been proven by scientists that animals can reduce our stress levels).

6. Name five things you can see, four things you can touch, three things you can hear, two things you can smell and one thing you can taste.

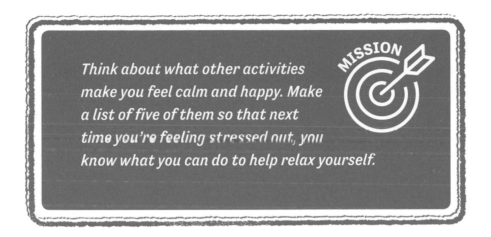

Think about what other activities make you feel calm and happy. Make a list of five of them so that next time you're feeling stressed out, you know what you can do to help relax yourself.

Being clear about what I couldn't control made a big difference when it came to managing my emotions before I went on stage. But what also helped me was just doing it. The more I got up on stage, the more I got used to it. It got easier. Some of that was because I got better at the technique of speaking in public. I learned when to pause and when to keep the story-telling going. And I learned (the hard way) when – and when not – to make jokes. The rest came from the fact that every time I walked out in front of the audience I was that bit more familiar with the emotions I was feeling. When the butterflies started leaping around in my stomach I could identify them as nerves. I knew how they affected me, and I knew what I could do to calm them.

Every time I did this, the hold my emotions had over me shrank a little more. Because every second you spend in the company of an emotion is a second spent learning how to control it.

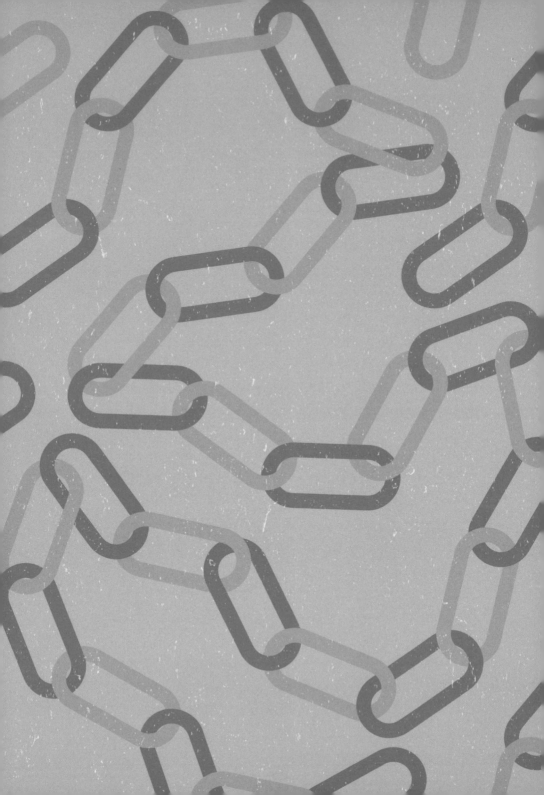

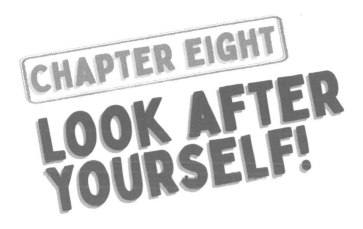

CHAPTER EIGHT
LOOK AFTER YOURSELF!

I'm going to have to start this chapter with a warning. *A lot of what follows is suspiciously similar to advice your parents would give you.* However, embarrassing as it is to admit this, it doesn't make what I'm going to say any less true.

RESILIENCE ISN'T JUST A MENTAL QUALITY.

THERE'S A VERY STRONG CONNECTION BETWEEN

OUR BODIES AND OUR MINDS.

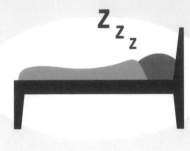

The food you eat, the amount of sleep you get, the exercise you take, and your relationships with other people – all of those things make a difference.

Our bodies are amazing. They produce 25 million new cells every second. Pound for pound, our bones are stronger than steel. When we're awake, our brains throw out enough energy to power a lightbulb. They're incredible, right?

But we take them for granted. And we neglect them. Imagine how much better we'd feel if we treated our bodies with as much attention as we do a new iPhone! When I go on adventures, like climbing Everest, I know that I'll only be able to withstand the demands of the expeditions if I invest effort in my physical and mental well-being. If I'm tired because I've stayed up too late, or am low on energy because I've been eating nothing but fried chicken and chocolate bars, I know I'm not going to be able to perform to the best of my abilities.

And that's still true now. If I'm feeling less than 100 per cent physically, then it drags me down mentally too. My brain is slow and unresponsive, I'm tense and snappy. I feel vulnerable, less able to deal with challenging emotions or situations. That's why I look after my mind and my body.

None of what I'll recommend over the following pages is extreme or unusual. I don't want you to feel you have to run marathons, or start diets where you're only allowed to eat peas. And it's fine to sometimes slob out in front of the TV with a giant tub of ice cream. (See, I bet your parents wouldn't say that.)

I just want you to realise that **the better care you take of yourself, the better you'll be able to withstand everything,** from the stress that comes with doing a difficult test at school, to those curveballs that have a nasty habit of landing on us when we least expect them.

EAT YOUR GREENS (BUT NOT JUST GREENS)!

There's a reason why athletes eat healthily: they want to be able to perform at their highest level. Now, of course I'm not saying you should be following the kinds of highly specialised nutritional regime they often do. But there is a proven connection between the food we put into our bodies and our mental health. Our diet can even affect our quality of sleep!

I don't need to tell you that it's not a good idea to have a burger and chips washed down with a gallon of fizzy drink for dinner every night, but faddy diets are just as unhealthy for you. Never eating pasta and bread, or just having cabbage soup at each meal isn't going to help anybody. You need to eat a balanced diet that has lots of fruits and vegetables, and contains a mix of carbohydrates, protein and fat. There's no one food that will ever give you all the nutrients you need.

If you do this, you'll feel happier and healthier, and you'll have more energy. What's not to like?

GET YOUR HEART GOING!

Exercise is brilliant. I couldn't imagine my life without it. It's not just that it helps keep you super-fit and full of energy:

WHEN YOU EXERCISE, **YOU'RE** BOOSTING **YOUR** HEALTH IN A MILLION **WAYS,** BUT YOU'RE ALSO SUPER-CHARGING YOUR HAPPINESS.

Exercise releases endorphins – the chemicals in your brain that help lift your mood and fight off anxiety and depression. It improves your sleep, helps build up your long-term health and will even make your memory better. And that's before we talk about the benefits of going outside into the fresh air, or the social benefits of taking part in activities with other people.

It can also be . . . fun.

Even if you don't normally think of yourself as sporty, you shouldn't make the mistake of thinking that exercise has to be a form of punishment. You don't have to force yourself to lift weights or go on epic runs. Just find something that you enjoy and that you can fit into your normal life, otherwise you'll find it really hard to stick at it. It doesn't matter what you do – dancing, tennis, cycling, climbing, swimming – as long as you're working hard enough that you can feel your heart beating faster, your breathing getting quicker and your body feeling warmer.

MISSION

Sometimes we might want to be a bit more active, and yet because we have busy lives it can be hard to koop up that exercise. We might have the best of intentions, but then we get to the end of the week and our days have been so full that we haven't managed to go for the bike ride we'd been looking forward to. One thing that I find helps is making physical activity part of my routine. I plan in advance when I'm going to do that bit of exercise and make sure that I keep a block of time free. I also think about whether I need to go to anywhere special to do it, and whether I need any equipment. I then try to do the same thing at the same time every week, so that it becomes a habit.

Think about what kind of exercise you'd like to do, then try to answer the questions below.

What do you want to do?

When can you do it?

Where can you do it?

What do you need to do it?

GET A GOOD NIGHT'S SLEEP . . . EVERY NIGHT!

Sleep is also brilliant! When we sleep, we're not just having cool dreams about winning the 100-metre gold medal at the Olympics, or hanging out with dinosaurs, we're also giving our poor over-worked bodies a chance to recover. Think about how much your body does for you every single day. While we sleep, we rest, digest and make the repairs needed after all that activity. **The more sleep we get, the more energy we'll have the next day and the better we'll be at concentrating and fighting off illness.** Good sleep aids the healing of injuries and improves our ability to manage stress. It also makes a massive difference to our brain's ability to function properly.

You'll realise the impact sleep has on you when you don't get enough. Your mind feels as if it's full of fog: you find it hard to focus or make good decisions. You'll be bad-tempered and difficult to be around, and you will be much more likely to be upset about small things. So, as tempting as it might be to stay up all night playing Minecraft, you will only be cheating yourself if you don't get enough sleep.

The annoying thing is that sleep isn't always straightforward. If you are struggling, why not try to follow these suggestions.

TIPS FOR GETTING GREAT SLEEP!

1. No screens an hour before bed. If you're watching television or messing about on your phone before you hit the sack, your brain will have been flooded with blue light, which sounds cool, but actually means that you've tricked your brain into thinking it's still daytime. Instead of getting ready to switch off, it's full of buzzing energy.

2. Have a window slightly open (ventilation is good for sleep!).

3. Avoid caffeine or fizzy drinks in the lead-up to bedtime.

4. Try to do a calming activity before going to sleep. Perhaps you could write in your diary or read a book. Or why not have a nice relaxing bath?

5. Always try to wake up at the same time each morning.

> *Next time you sleep badly (whether that's struggling to get to sleep, or waking up in the middle of the night) try to make a note of what you did before going to bed. Do the same next time you sleep really well. Compare those lists. What could you do differently in the future to ensure you get your ten hours of shut-eye?*

MISSION

BE WARY OF THE UNREAL WORLD OF SOCIAL MEDIA!

Social media can be great. It allows us to connect with friends and strangers in amazing ways that people even a decade ago couldn't have dreamed of. But if we have an unhealthy relationship with social media, then it can have a negative impact on our mental resilience.

It can be the opposite of the internal confidence we talked about in Chapter 3. It creates an unreal world in which our view of ourselves and our own worth is entirely dependent on how many followers we have, how many people like our posts and what people say about us in the comments.

You don't need me to tell you spending too much time in that unreal world is a bad idea. And you don't need me to tell you that if you base your self-esteem on the reactions you get on social media, you can become incredibly vulnerable. It's like building a house on quicksand. When you're growing up, and are still finding who you are, it's so easy to feel undermined by strong opinions from other people who seem to know more than you do.

So while there are many great things about social media, be very careful about your relationship with it. Most people are nice, like you. They want to chat to their friends and make new ones. But there is a minority who don't think like that and say hurtful things on purpose. It can be terribly distressing when you are the subject of online abuse.

What you must always remember is that the only reason that this minority do this to other people is because they can. It's NOTHING to do with you, your looks or your personality. And it's EVERYTHING to do with the fact that they're bored and feel inadequate. There's no deep reason for their behaviour beyond the fact that they have literally nothing better to do with their lives other than bully and hurt people.

Which means that there is nothing you could ever say or do that would make them stop. There's no photo you could post, or message you could write, that could change their minds. They're attention-seekers, it's not personal. They don't know the real you, and therefore there's no reason to be troubled by any of their insults, no matter how cruel they might sound. All they want is a reaction, because that's what they feed off. Don't respond to them in any way. Just ignore them, shut your phone or computer down and walk out of the room. The chances are that by the time you've reached the door, they'll already have scuttled off to pollute some other corner of the internet. Think of them as a digital equivalent of the spiteful critics we talked about in Chapter 4.

Online bullying by people you know – perhaps kids from your school, or who live nearby – can feel even more upsetting. But you don't have to go through this alone. The bullies might have a problem (believe me, they definitely have a problem), but that doesn't mean you have to suffer too. Even if what they're saying or doing is making you feel miserable for thirty seconds, that's thirty seconds too long.

It doesn't matter if it's happening now, or is something that took place in the past. Speak up. **Tell an adult who you trust. Or you could call Childline on 0800 1111. Calls are free, confidential and their lines are manned 24/7, so there will always be somebody to speak to.**

YOU DON'T HAVE TO DO THIS ALONE!

After reading this book I want you to feel as if you're able to deal with lots of things yourself, without needing to always be asking a parent or friend for help or support. That's important. Being able to rely on your own resources and strength is an amazing advantage to have in life. But I don't want you to feel as if you have to fix everything on your own.

TALKING TO OTHERS ABOUT YOUR PROBLEMS OR FEARS IS ABSOLUTELY ESSENTIAL TO FEELING EMOTIONALLY STRONG AND SUPPORTED.

I also think anybody who opens up about the things that are troubling them is incredibly brave. You must remember that as fast as you are growing, you're still a kid. You should never feel as if you have to carry the weight of the world on your shoulders. The adults in your life (whether they're parents, teachers, an aunt, an uncle or a grandparent) want you to be independent, they want you to thrive in your own right, but they also care for you and want to be there to help when you need it.

It's a very old cliché, but a problem shared really can be a problem halved. Other people can offer you advice and support. They can be a great shoulder to cry on. And they also offer different perspectives. When you talk to another human being about something, the chances are that they will see it a completely different way from you. That can really help on those occasions when you're faced by those tricky problems that you just can't work out how to solve yourself.

Be resilient, be strong, be brave, but never be afraid of confiding in others, or asking for help.

MISSION

You don't have to climb Everest or ace your exams to be making progress towards becoming the best possible version of you. Never underestimate the impact that small achievements can have on your sense of well-being. I feel so much better on those mornings when I've got up early, had a shower, cleaned my teeth and put on fresh clothes. All those little steps add up, they make you feel good about yourself and help to build motivation and momentum. If you start your day off with a positive act, no matter how tiny, you'll want to follow it with another because it feels so good.

What little steps can you take to make sure you begin every day feeling full of energy and positivity?

CHAPTER NINE

THERE'S NO SUCH THING AS PERFECT (AND THAT'S FINE)

We're all works in progress. I know that must feel especially true for you at the moment. You're at an age where everything is changing. Your body and your mind are growing at an insane rate. And the demands that are placed on you are getting tougher. School is getting harder, and maybe some social stuff is getting a tiny bit trickier to work out too.

I remember that when I was a kid, I was convinced of two things:

1.   That I was the only person in the world who sometimes felt a bit overwhelmed by life.

2.   That one day I'd understand everything. I'd be good at everything. I'd have everything worked out. I would be Master of the Universe (OK, I was getting a bit carried away there).

I was completely wrong about both. It's so easy to convince yourself that everybody except you is doing brilliantly, coasting serenely through life. What I learned as I grew older is that almost all of us struggle from time to time, and most of us have moments when we feel overwhelmed. It's just that, for one reason or another, people rarely talk about it.

I also learned that we never reach a point when we can sit back and tell ourselves that we've got everything worked out. Now, I can see that doesn't sound ideal, but for me understanding this fact was a massively liberating experience. Because when you realise that perfection doesn't exist, and that nobody's perfect (not you, not me, not anybody), then suddenly you realise that you've got space to get things the wrong way round, or to mess up, or to (occasionally) do stupid stuff. And it doesn't mean you're unusual, it just means you're a human!

MISSION

Our friends aren't perfect either. Think about your best friend. You hang about with them all the time, you chat and have loads of fun. But sometimes you might find them a bit annoying.

Take a couple of moments to think about the things you like about them . . . and also the ways in which these qualities can sometimes end up frustrating you.

It could be something like this . . .

My friend is super creative and has an amazing imagination. I love how she always ends up doing wacky, spontaneous things, but this can mean she sometimes lets me down last minute because she has got involved in something suddenly. She can also be a bit disorganised and forgets stuff. But I know she doesn't do it to be mean and she cares deeply for me, and most of the time she's the best person in the world to be around!

When I was a kid, I was the best in my school at athletics. This isn't me boasting, I really was! I could run faster and jump further than anybody else, even though I was still quite small. Winning all the events at sports day year after year was what gave me my confidence.

But then one year disaster struck. A new boy had started a couple of weeks before sports day. I didn't know very much about him. He was sort of a mystery. Until, that is, he whizzed past me during the 100 metres. He beat me and I was devastated, because it had been so important to me that I was the fastest kid in my year.

It wasn't until a few weeks after the race that I realised how wrong I had been. The truth is, you're never going to be the best at everything all the time. You can't win every race. There will always be people who are faster, or cleverer, or better at playing the piano than you are.

And you're inevitably going to have bad days, or have moments when you're unlucky. There's always going to be stuff happening that's completely out of your control.

The experience taught me that if you always insist on perfection, you're guaranteeing you'll never be happy. If you think that you're a failure if you're not top of the class every time there's a test, you're setting yourself targets that are impossible to reach. Once you can accept that you won't always get things right, and that there are things about you that aren't perfect, then life becomes a lot more straightforward.

'BUT,' you might ask, 'if perfection isn't possible, is there any point in trying?'

'Yes,' I would reply.
'Abso-flipping-lutely.'

Because the important thing isn't that you're perfect. The important thing is that you're getting better. We're really bad at recognising incremental improvements – those tiny steps forward we're making all the time.

You're pretty unlikely to get 100 per cent in your next French test, but you can try your hardest to make sure you do better than last time. So when you're thinking about what sort of progress you've been able to make as you've been reading this book, don't ask yourself: Am I the most resilient kid in the world? **Ask: Am I a bit more resilient than I was yesterday?**

You have probably been better than you think at getting better. *Try to think of three things you've improved at over the last six months.*

MISSION

But don't stop there! *Next list three things you want to improve in the future.*

If you can manage just one of them, then you're already one step closer to completing Mission Total Resilience.

What is also hugely unrealistic and unhelpful is spending your life comparing yourself to others. Especially since the comparisons we make are almost always unfair. Generally, we set somebody else's best quality against what we see as our worst quality. It's as if we're playing a game in which the rules are biased against us!

SO MUCH BETTER THAN ME!

I'M NOT AS GOOD AS THAT!

TOP MARKS

That's just as true of celebrities on the TV as it is of that girl who lives down the street who is always talking about how great she is. We look at other people and their achievements and beat ourselves up because we aren't famous, or didn't get picked for the school basketball team like our friend did. But why would you want to be so hard on yourself? What good will it do? Being jealous of your friend isn't going to make you any more likely to play in the next game. It'll just make you sad and maybe even bitter too. A much better use of your time and energy would be focusing on what you can do yourself to improve your skills. You CAN'T change how well your friend plays (unless you steal her trainers, which you don't need me to tell you would be a pretty horrible thing to do). You CAN change how well you play.

BEST PAINTER

The fact that the new kid was faster than me in that one race didn't make me a bad runner. I was so wrapped up in my disappointment at having lost my position as the fastest kid at school

FASTEST RUNNER

that I overlooked the fact that I'd run my quickest-ever time. I should have been happy! I'd done something better than I'd ever done it before! Instead, I robbed myself of the pleasure of enjoying my achievement. That kid's performance should have been irrelevant to me; mine was the only one that mattered.

But on that day, I'd forgotten something really important. **Life isn't a competition. Comparing yourself to other people will only make you unhappy and disappointed.** You won't win every prize, you're never going to be the best at everything. Perfection just isn't possible.

THE TRUTH IS THAT YOU CAN ONLY BE THE BEST VERSION OF YOU.

AND THAT IS MORE THAN ENOUGH.

CHAPTER TEN

THE TEN STEPS TO TOTAL RESILIENCE

1. ACKNOWLEDGE THAT BAD THINGS WILL HAPPEN

I think the world is an amazing place full of excitement and fun opportunities. But sometimes life goes really wrong. Or you just have to do stuff that you find unpleasant or challenging, like maths tests. If you pretend these things don't exist, you'll never be able to prepare yourself for that moment when you do have to face them (and you will).

2. YOU'RE RESILIENT ALREADY, AND THE ONLY WAY IS UP!

You're probably already much tougher and more capable than you realise. Think of the many tough experiences you've survived already. But it's possible to build and build on that resilience until you become a resilience superhero!

3. WORK ON WHAT YOU CAN CONTROL, DON'T WORRY ABOUT WHAT YOU CAN'T

We all waste far too much time being anxious about stuff that's completely out of our hands. It's much better to focus all your attention and effort on what you CAN control.

4. BUILD A CORE OF INTERNAL CONFIDENCE THAT NOBODY CAN TAKE AWAY FROM YOU

Nobody was born confident, but everybody can become confident. Especially you. And when you prove to yourself over and again what you're capable of, you'll have built a foundation of confidence that almost nothing can shake.

5. TAKE (LITTLE) STEPS OUTSIDE YOUR COMFORT ZONE

You'll never be able to grow or get stronger if you're not willing to step outside your comfort zone. Test yourself, stretch yourself, and open yourself up to new experiences. I promise it will be worth it.

6. YOU CAN CONTROL YOUR FEAR

There isn't a single human being on the planet who is fearless. Not even me! None of us will ever be able to banish fear. And yet it is possible (and actually quite straightforward) to learn how to control it.

7. LEARN TO EMBRACE FAILURE

Behind almost every success are a thousand failures. Failure isn't what you do instead of success, it's what you do on the way to success. So stop seeing failure as a disastrous dead end, and start treating is as a brilliant opportunity to learn and grow.

8. MAKE FRIENDS WITH YOUR EMOTIONS!

Whonever you experience an emotion – whether
it's happiness, or anger, or fear – take a moment
to reflect on what you're feeling and why.
The more you know about your emotions and
the effect they have on you, the more control
you'll be able to exert over them.

9. TAKE CARE OF YOUR BODY AND YOUR BODY WILL TAKE CARE OF YOU

Your body and mind aren't separate. They're
really closely connected. So if you eat well,
sleep well and take enough exercise, you're
building an amazing foundation that will help
you and your emotions stand up to even the
most challenging situations.

Z
Z
Z

10. REMEMBER THAT NOBODY, REPEAT NOBODY, IS PERFECT

And this is OK! Instead of worrying about making mistakes, or comparing yourself to other people, just focus on being a bit better than you were the day before.

I don't expect you to remember this all at once. There might be some steps that you want to come back to later. Don't worry.

RESILLYENCE

RESILIENS

RISILENCE

RESILLIENCE

RESILIENCE

BEING RESILIENT ISN'T ABOUT GETTING EVERYTHING RIGHT ALL THE TIME.

And it's not about being amazingly competent immediately. Life isn't like a computer game — you can't complete it. But that doesn't matter. Actually, it's a flipping good thing. You can keep on getting better and stronger all the time. There's no need to ever stop. You've got almost endless chances to pick up cool new skills. You've got the opportunity to try a million things until you find the one thing you love. You've got space to get stuff wrong. You've got time to pick yourself up all over again . . .

WHAT ARE YOU WAITING FOR?
GO FOR IT!

THE MISSIONS

You can read *Mission: Total Resilience* in whatever order you want. And there might be some chapters you want to return to when you're facing a specific challenge or task. To remind you of the key lessons from each chapter, I've collected all the missions that appear throughout the book together in one place. You can work through them whenever and however suits you. And remember that even if you manage to finish only one, you're still making progress!

MISSION 1 (PAGE 20)

We should never underestimate the importance of our family and friends. They help us celebrate the happy moments in life. But they also can help us get through the times that feel tough or challenging.

Take a couple of moments to consider the people who support and believe in you. Then try to think of ways that you can show them how much you appreciate everything they do.

MISSION 2 (PAGES 26-27)

When we're faced by situations that feel tough or upsetting it can seem overwhelming. But there's an exercise you can do to get your thoughts flowing in a different direction.

1. Ask yourself, How are you feeling?
When I was a kid in France I was afraid that people would laugh at me if I stumbled and made mistakes while trying to speak French.

2. Name what that worry makes you want to do.
All I wanted to do was hide in my den away from everybody else.

The exciting bit is what comes next. This is where you can change that negative thought into a positive one.

3. Instead of imagining a disaster scenario, try to imagine what it would look like if things went well.
For me that was telling myself, I'll try speaking a bit of French and people will cheer me for doing my best and giving it a go.

4. How do you feel when you've adopted this positive perspective?
It made me feel much more happy and confident. I was actually quite excited about trying out a few words.

Spend a couple of minutes thinking about stuff that would normally leave you feeling anxious. See what happens if you change the way you look at it. Swap a negative outcome for a positive one. Try to make this an automatic habit – always imagining a positive scenario rather than a negative one. Then you'll have equipped yourself with an amazing tool that will help you whenever things begin to feel a bit tricky or too much to cope with. And if doing this feels hard at first, ask someone you trust to help you think about it.

MISSION 3 (PAGE 36)

I don't care who you are or where you're from or what you've done. I don't care how clever you are, or how tall, or what colour your hair is. None of that matters. You've already got a core of resilience inside you. I'm not just saying this to make you feel better. Remember, I'm the big chief instructor, I'm tough, I tell it like it is. I'm saying it because it's true.

Here's a quick test. Think back over the last couple of years. Make a list of five things that you've found tricky or have upset you. It doesn't matter if they're big or small. Maybe it was missing your friends during lockdown, or one of your favourite pets died, or perhaps it was a teacher shouting at you for messing about.

Do you know what connects all these things (apart from that they happened to you)? YOU SURVIVED THEM! You might not have enjoyed them. They might have made you unhappy or sad. But you got through them. That proves you already are resilient.

MISSION 4 (PAGE 38)

Next time something unfamiliar or challenging approaches, draw strength by thinking of something you've done that made you really proud. What skills did you use? What does it tell you about how strong and capable you already are?

MISSION 5 (PAGE 40)

We're our own worst critics and we're not always able to highlight what we're good at. But the people around us are often much better at seeing how much we're capable of.

Step out of your shoes for a moment and try to imagine what a grown-up – like a parent or one of your teachers, or any adult you respect and admire – would say you can do well. Does this change your own view of your abilities?

MISSION 6 (PAGE 43)

Ask yourself, what can you do now that you couldn't last year?

Were you good at it the first time around, or did you need to take a couple of goes at it?

MISSION 7 (PAGE 52)

Think about something that you really want to try, but that you're a bit nervous about doing. Write that activity down, and also all the reasons why you feel nervous about doing it.

MISSION 8 (PAGE 55)

Remember the new thing you wanted to try that you wrote down (see MISSION 7, page 52)? That's the big mission.

Try to think about a few of the little missions you can easily do to help you get ready for the big mission. Make a list. They can be really small – but everything you do will be a positive step forward. What's the first thing that you can do?

MISSION 9 (PAGE 59)

When I was a soldier and I got anxious, I'd take a moment to remind myself of all the stages I'd had to get through to be where I was. All the tests I'd passed, the challenges I'd overcome. It wasn't a question of being big-headed, it was just about being honest. And it really helped. I had earned the right to be there.

It's too easy to focus on what you can't do. What we don't do enough of is record and celebrate all the things we can do.

When you're learning something new, why not keep a record of it. You could put it up in your bedroom, or on the fridge door. And if you can't think of something yourself, why not ask a teacher or parent for suggestions. Remember, other people are sometimes better at spotting your progress than you are!

MISSION 10 (PAGE 68)

Ask yourself how you can make everyday tasks and chores a tiny bit harder. Maybe you could time yourself as you do your geography homework, or you could try a trickier bit of music when you're practising the piano.

MISSION 11 (PAGE 69)

Try to get into the habit of finding solutions to tricky situations. Think about what you would do if . . .

1. You tripped up while running a race.

2. You walked into the wrong classroom by mistake.

3. You saw your friend being bullied.

MISSION 12 (PAGE 71)

There's no shame in finding something difficult. That just means you're stretching yourself. You're becoming a better version of you! But if you're trying something new and you feel your will to carry on ebbing away, try to do these two things:

1. Think about how good it would feel if you didn't give up.

2. Think about how disappointing it would be if you did give up. Maybe there have already been times when you've been doing something hard and considering giving up, but carried on. How did that make you feel?

MISSION 13 (PAGE 74)

It's helpful to be able to tell the difference between constructive and negative feedback.

Read the two examples below, then think about the ways in which they're different.

'Jack, I liked your enthusiasm there. Just try to listen right to the end of the instruction before getting up to do the task. Otherwise you might miss something you need to know.'

'Jack, you got that all wrong. You've got to do better next time.'

Which comment is helpful and which is unhelpful and not constructive? How would you feel if a teacher said them to you?

MISSION 14 (PAGE 82)

Make a list of three things that you'd like to do but are afraid to try. What is it that makes you nervous?

MISSION 15 (PAGE 87)

Let's draw a body map! Spend a couple of minutes thinking about how being anxious or afraid makes all the different parts of your body feel. Then write them all down.

For example, you could write something like this . . .

Stomach: tingly
Legs: jiggly
Mouth: dry

MISSION 16 (PAGE 94)

Think about a fear you have currently. Write down how you could gradually reduce the power it has over you. (Make sure you include little rewards along the way so that you can celebrate how far you've come!) Try to imagine how strong and confident you'll feel once you've finally conquered that anxiety. For instance, if you're worried about performing in public, take a deep breath and visualise stepping onto the stage. You've practised hard, you've learned your lines and you feel confident. So confident, in fact, that you give everyone a big smile!

How does this exercise make you feel?

MISSION 17 (PAGE 103)

What lesson would you learn if you were late for school because you hadn't packed your bag the night before?

What would you do differently next time?

MISSION 18 (PAGE 106)

Try to think of three times in your life, or the lives of your family and friends, when stuff that initially seemed like a failure actually ended up becoming an opportunity.

MISSION 19 (PAGES 108-109)

Here are two situations where I made a bit of a mess of things. If you need to refresh your memory, it's OK to flick back through chapter six! See pages 110-11 to see what I ended up doing.

What would you do to respond to these failures if you were in my shoes? Is there anything there that you could transform into an opportunity?

Q1. A friend let me down by not turning up for something when he'd promised he would. Before I'd given the situation any thought I sent him an angry text message. This hurt his feelings and we got into an argument and didn't speak to each other for a bit. (Don't worry, we're pals again now!)

Q2. When I was a young soldier I wanted to test myself by joining the elite Parachute Regiment. The problem was that I kept struggling during the endurance test that was part of the selection process. We had to do these really long runs carrying rucksacks that were full of weights. It was hard for me because my legs were a bit shorter than all the other recruits'. Every time we went on one of these runs, I came last. It really felt to me as if I was failing. I was at risk of being thrown off the course.

MISSION 20 (PAGE 116)

Think of a situation that would usually make you feel stressed. Now list three things about it you can control, and three things about it you can't control.

How does completing this mission change the way you feel about that stressful situation?

MISSION 21 (PAGE 123)

Think about what other activities make you feel calm and happy. Make a list of five of them so that next time you're feeling stressed out, you know what you can do to help relax yourself.

MISSION 22 (PAGE 131)

Sometimes we might want to be a bit more active, and yet because we have busy lives it can be hard to keep up that exercise. We might have the best of intentions, but then we get to the end of the week and our days have been so full that we haven't managed to go for the bike ride we'd been looking forward to. One thing that I find helps is making physical activity part of my routine. I plan in advance when I'm going to do that bit of exercise and make sure that I keep a block of time free. I also think about whether I need to go to anywhere special to do it, and whether I need any equipment. I then try to do the same thing at the same time every week, so that it becomes a habit.

Think about what kind of exercise you'd like to do, then try to answer the following questions:

What do you want to do?

When can you do it?

Where can you do it?

What do you need to do it?

MISSION 23 (PAGE 134)

Next time you sleep badly (whether that's struggling to get to sleep, or waking up in the middle of the night) try to make a note of what you did before going to bed. Do the same next time you sleep really well. Compare those lists. What could you do differently in the future to ensure you get your ten hours of shut-eye?

MISSION 24 (PAGE 139)

You don't have to climb Everest or ace your exams to be making progress towards becoming the best possible version of you. Never underestimate the impact that small achievements can have on your sense of well-being. I feel so much better on those mornings when I've got up early, had a shower, cleaned my teeth and put on fresh clothes. All those little steps add up, they make you feel good about yourself and help to build motivation and momentum. If you start your day off with a positive act, no matter how tiny, you'll want to follow it with another because it feels so good.

What little steps can you take to make sure you begin every day feeling full of energy and positivity?

MISSION 25 (PAGE 143)

Our friends aren't perfect either. Think about your best friend. You hang about with them all the time, you chat and have loads of fun. But sometimes you might find them a bit annoying.

Take a couple of moments to think about the things you like about them . . . and also the ways in which these qualities can sometimes end up frustrating you.

It could be something like this . . .

My friend is super creative and has an amazing imagination. I love how she always ends up doing wacky, spontaneous things, but this can mean she sometimes lets me down last minute because she has got involved in something suddenly. She can also be a bit disorganised and forgets stuff.

But I know she doesn't do it to be mean and she cares deeply for me, and most of the time she's the best person in the world to be around!

MISSION 26 (PAGE 147)

You have probably been better than you think at getting better. ***Try to think of three things you've improved at over the last six months.***

But don't stop there! ***Next list three things you want to improve in the future.***

If you can manage just one of them, then you're already one step closer to completing Mission Total Resilience.

ANT MIDDLETON is an adventurer, public speaker and television presenter. He is the author of five *Sunday Times* no. 1 bestsellers, *First Man In*, *The Fear Bubble*, *Cold Justice*, *Zero Negativity* and *Mental Fitness*. His books have sold over 1.8 million copies around the world. When he's not climbing Mt Everest, or jumping out of helicopters, he likes to spend time with his wife and children.

Consultant **DR MIQUELA WALSH**, DEdPsych, MsC (Dist), BSc (Hons), HCPC accredited, is an Educational Psychologist who supports children and young people with a range of emotional, social, and learning needs.